Modernization without Revolution
Lebanon's Experience

INTERNATIONAL DEVELOPMENT RESEARCH CENTER
Indiana University

Directors:
George J. Stolnitz, 1966-1972
William J. Siffin, 1972——

Studies in Development

NO. 1
WORLD POPULATION—THE VIEW AHEAD
(ed.) Richard N. Farmer, John D. Long, George J. Stolnitz

NO. 2
SOCIALIST MANAGEMENT AND PLANNING:
TOPICS IN COMPARATIVE SOCIALIST ECONOMICS
By Nicolas Spulber

NO. 3
THE UN AND THE PALESTINIAN REFUGEES:
A STUDY IN NONTERRITORIAL ADMINISTRATION
By Edward H. Buehrig

NO. 4
SOVIET AND EAST EUROPEAN FOREIGN TRADE: (1946-1969)
A STATISTICAL COMPENDIUM
By Paul Marer

NO. 5
RURAL POLITICS AND SOCIAL CHANGE IN THE MIDDLE EAST
(ed.) Richard Antoun, Iliya Harik

NO. 6
MODERNIZATION WITHOUT REVOLUTION: LEBANON'S EXPERIENCE
By Elie Adib Salem

Elie Adib Salem

Modernization without Revolution
Lebanon's Experience

Indiana University Press
Bloomington & London

Copyright © 1973 by Indiana University Press
All rights reserved

No part of this book may be reproduced or utilized in any form or by any means, electronic or mechanical, including photocopying and recording, or by any information storage and retrieval system, without permission in writing from the publisher. The Association of American University Presses' Resolution on Permissions constitutes the only exception to this prohibition.

Published in Canada by Fitzhenry and Whiteside Limited, Don Mills, Ontario

Library of Congress catalogue card number: 72-85854
ISBN: 0-253-33870-0
Manufactured in the United States of America

To my parents
Adib and Lamia Salem

CONTENTS

Foreword	xi
Preface	xiii
Introduction	1
I / Forces for Change: Past and Present	5
The Cultural Context—Historical Forces Leading to Modernization—Post-Independence Factors	
II / The Communal Society—Modernization under Laissez-Faire	18
Land and Climate—Population—Confessional Groupings—Emigration—Rural-Urban Distribution and Comparisons—Education—Economy—Summary	
III / Lebanon's Political Formula: Governing by Consensus	52
Za'īm Club—Military Club—Ecclesiastic Club—Embassy Club—Business Club—Intellectual Club—	
IV / Bureaucracy in Transition	75
Distribution and Relation to Political Formula—Characteristics of Upper Bureaucracy—Bottleneck Problems—Reform—Summary	

V / Planning and Non-Planning:
     The Lebanese Compromise   107
       *Planning Mechanism—Plans—Planning
       Effectiveness*
VI / Prospects for the Communal
     Society   138
NOTES   146
INDEX   171

TABLES

TABLE 2.1 1970 Population, 1963–1970 Growth Rate, Area, and Density of Eight Middle East Countries 21

TABLE 2.2 Distribution by Industry Sector of Labor Force and G.N.P. (1966–69 Average Percentages) 42

TABLE 2.3 Distribution of Craft Establishments into Five or More Workers (1969) 46

TABLE 2.4 Value and Index Numbers of Industrial Production (1965–67) 47

TABLE 2.5 Distribution of Landowners and Cultivated Area by Size (1950s) 49

TABLE 3.1 Occupational Distribution of Deputies in Seven Lebanese Parliaments for Selected Years, 1943–1964 58

TABLE 4.1 Distribution of Lebanese Civil Service by Ministry 1965 and 1969 77

TABLE 5.1 Estimated Cost of the 1958 Five-Year Plan 116–118

TABLE 5.2 Table of the Development Projects and Their Cost (1965–1969 Plan) 122–125

FOREWORD

Professor Salem's study contributes a case history to our knowledge of modernization processes and offers something more. It provides the rationale for a new category in the taxonomy of planning and development. It adds something to the old dichotomy of "plan or no plan" and to the more recent array of experiences with fragmentary, aborted, misdirected, abruptly re-directed and/or only tenuously implemented national plans for achieving large-scale socio-economic change: we may now with reason begin to speak of "planned planlessness."

In Lebanon this approach has evolved into a fine art. Planning has been less a method for advancing the future than a device for allaying it, less the tool of a polity mobilizing to pursue new goals than a front for preserving old ones. Despite an explicit set of development targets, and sizable administrative machinery, individual and public decision-making continue much as if there were no plan at all.

That planning may serve a government for ulterior purposes, or even as a front, is hardly surprising, given planning's profound political implications. The distinctiveness of the Lebanese experience is the directness of its linkages with very long-standing conservative political traditions, dating well back into the previous century. Here those linkages are documented by a trained observer having the exceptional entrée of an "insider." The value of such special access is especially apparent in the discussion of the bureaucracy and the uniquely Lebanese institution of "clubs."

The reader will also find authoritative accounts of more conventional themes. One concerns the deep historical roots of Lebanon's dualistic society and the ways that dualism affects development in all of its main facets. The confessional character of Lebanese dualism adds something distinctive to a subject of significance throughout the "third world." Professor Salem's updated demographic, social, and economic profiles for Lebanon will be appreciated by anyone familiar with the problems of finding, let alone interpreting, statistical documentation concerning that country or, for that matter, practically any part of the Middle East.

The present volume, sixth in the series of Studies in Development issued by the International Development Research Center, reflects the Center's continuing interest in planning-development interrelations. Other IDRC efforts, past and in process, focus on this subject, which we continue to regard as a key one in development research.

August, 1972   George J. Stolnitz
DIRECTOR, IDRC, 1966–1972

PREFACE

I have worked on this book over the past four years. Initially I had intended to concentrate on the planning process, but found myself directed into a study of the political, economic, and social forces that have led to the modernization of Lebanon. Naturally, and as it were, humbly, the planning process assumed its proper place as one of a number of processes involved in the modernization of this country.

Lebanon is a country where one's first impressions are often proved wrong: it has been described as "precarious," "improbable," and as a "mosaic," but the flexibility of its system, the experience and shrewdness of its leaders, and the stability of its institutions have surprised all observers. My own impressions have changed since I began writing this book.

Many people helped in the completion of this work, and to list them all would incur the sin of omission. I must acknowledge my gratitude to the International Development Research Center at Indiana University for its generous support and sponsorship, to the Department of Political Science at Indiana University, and to the Center of Middle East Studies at the American University of Beirut. To my distinguished colleagues in these institutions I owe more than I can adequately express. I am particularly indebted to Dr. George Stolnitz, former Director of the International Development Research Center, for his critical advice and continuous guidance. My colleagues at the IDRC offered useful criticism, and members of the staff helped greatly in editing and typing. I wish also to thank friends in the Lebanese political, administrative, intellectual, and business fields for their patience in discussing issues with me and for valuable material that they have offered.

Particular thanks are due to my assistants Jihad Salem, Lili Milki, Maha Samara, and Dianna Blincoe, and to Nina Ghattas, who typed various versions of the manuscript.

During the past year my wife, Phyllis Sell Salem, assumed the impossible task of filling research gaps, putting the pieces together, and bringing the manuscript to completion. In a real sense this is her book, too, and she has kindly accepted the dubious honor of assuming joint responsibility for its flaws. All others are, of course, in no way responsible for any error in judgment or in fact.

E.A.S.

Modernization without Revolution
Lebanon's Experience

Introduction

Lebanon is among the most modernized countries in the Arab world. It is unusual among Third World countries in that its modernization has been brought about almost entirely by private endeavors; its government, committed to laissez-faire principles, has played little part in the modernization process. Lebanon has long had close economic and cultural contacts with Europe through trade, investment, missionary activities, and partly as a result, institutions of higher education which are largely based on a Western model. All these factors have contributed to the growth of a free market economy in Lebanon.

Lebanon's communal structure is unique, with approximately half of the population Muslim and the rest Christian. These groups have worked out a remarkably successful system of accommodation whereby government posts and policy decisions are shared on a roughly proportional basis. Competition, both political and economic, between sects and subsects is keen —and this has contributed to modernization—but it is usually peaceful.

Though ties with the West are centuries old, the foundations for a more intensive era of modernization were laid during the period of the French Mandate (1920–1943). The French introduced many Western ideas, institutions, and legal systems. At the same time, since World War I strong tides of political and ideological change have swept the Arab world, in which Lebanon has shared. A rising demand for more modernization, for economic development, and for bettering the conditions of the poor has made these goals prime objectives of Lebanese society and government.

The rise of military regimes in the Arab world, together with growing demands among the Lebanese for radical reform of the country's still strongly traditional institutions, has introduced new tensions. The political leadership, anxious to preserve a liberal, democratic, communal order and also to respond to the new demands, has attempted wide-ranging bureaucratic innovations and has instituted a form of development planning. Not all political leaders have fully supported these measures. Vested interests, confessional traditions, and Lebanese distrust of state initiatives have hindered reform and frustrated development efforts. Lebanon faces the dilemma of trying to preserve political liberty and a pluralistic society while at the same time mobilizing its resources to benefit the disadvantaged and the poor.

Elsewhere in the Arab world attempts to accelerate economic and social reforms have led to military or paramilitary regimes, generally accompanied by restrictions on political life. Lebanon's policy of gradual change by democratic methods, while preserving a traditional communalism, appears to be a gamble whose outcome will be watched with interest far beyond the country's borders.

Modernization is defined here as the process by which a country adapts, transforms, or replaces its traditional institutions and patterns of life under the influence of the new science and technology that arose during the Renaissance in western Europe and has since spread throughout the world. The literature of modernization focuses on rationalism, democracy, viable institutions, economic expansion, rising standards of living, and planned development of national resources. All of these elements, which overlap, will be treated in the following chapters.

Many Lebanese who support modernization have attended Western universities or Lebanese universities patterned on Western models; hence they have been strongly influenced by intellectual trends in Europe and America. No systematic or clear-cut ideology has, however, emerged among Lebanon's "modernizers," "reformers," or "new elite." Such people are found at top levels of government, in the bureaucracy, in academic life, and in private business. At the same time, many are unemployed or underemployed. Their principal forums are magazines, pamphlets, books, and the important though informal social and intellectual clubs.[1] In general they call for transcending local and confessional limitations, for encouragement of democratic institutions, for universal literacy, and for a scientific approach to curing social ills.[2]

Although many Arab intellectuals continue to hope that revolutionary governments will effect radical reforms, such hopes have often been disappointed. Indeed, the fact that so many Arab intellectuals and revolutionaries have elected to reside in Lebanon suggests that its liberal, communal order has many attractions throughout the Arab world. Lebanese intellectuals, as well, except for small groups on the extreme right and left, tend to prefer a liberal order, which they believe is adequate to accomplish rapid and far-reaching political, social, and economic reforms.

The aim of this book is to show how modernization has occurred within Lebanon's communal and pluralistic society, and how that society has developed successful institutions to ensure continuing modernization with a minimum of social and political strain and without resort to a radical ideology. The diversity of beliefs and attitudes in Lebanese society has furthered rather than hindered modernization. The slow gains accomplished, step by step, in cultural, economic, and political spheres are the result of stable political institutions and of a formula for government based on conciliation and consensus.

Lebanon thus differs from most other Arab countries of the Middle East, where modernization is being guided by military elites with radical ideological commitments. Lebanon's relative success shows that there are various routes to modernization, and that gradualism with political stability may be preferable to a radical but unstable regime.

This book is divided into six chapters. Chapter One deals with nineteenth- and twentieth-century movements toward Lebanese modernization. Chapter Two, which provides background information on demographic, economic, and educational trends, traces the process of modernization. Chapter Three examines the country's unique political formula for accommodating change. Chapter Four discusses the relationship of the bureaucracy to the political structure and its role in modernization. Chapter Five describes planning for modernization, and Chapter Six presents some conclusions and indicates alternative courses for the future.

The author has drawn extensively on personal background and experience, discussions with Lebanese intellectuals and leaders from other social sectors, reading of Lebanese and Arab writings, and the rapidly growing world literature on modernization and social change. The paucity of written material and of accurate up-to-date statistical data on some basic indicators of change has been a limiting factor. All parts of the book, however, have been checked by "insiders" in the political and bureaucratic mechanisms. This is, of course, no guarantee against faulty judgment on the part of the author.

1
Forces for Change: Past and Present

The Cultural Context

In Lebanon the past is very much alive. Long-time religious beliefs remain strong, the prevailing outlook is traditional, and ancient institutions still play a significant role in the lives of the majority of the population. The young Muslim wants to know how democracy, development, planning, etc., relate to Islam, and whether the Prophet has taken a stand on these questions. He seeks and often finds in the religion of Islam bases for evolving a philosophy of modernization.

The Christian Lebanese similarly are anxious to find historical and religious grounds for legitimizing change. They have found it easy, in theory, to identify with European interpretations of history and religion. However, as a small minority in the Arab world, they are continually engaged in intellectual interaction with Arabism and therefore, have found it necessary to relate also to strategic support points in Arabic culture. Western concepts need to be presented to the Arabs in a manner acceptable to Arabic culture by finding in that culture existing concepts which support modernization and change. Both Christian and Muslim Lebanese writers on modernization draw heavily on liberal Islamic interpretations, and particularly those relating to public interest. Arab history is widely searched for examples which can be used in developing Lebanese polity.

The Lebanese, irrespective of confessional origins, are necessarily aware that they live in the midst of the Arab world, which is over 90 percent Sunni Muslim. An Arab country, a member of the Arab League, and by virtue of the Muslim half of its population related to the larger Islamic World, Lebanon is the only country in the Middle East with a dual religious base. Lebanese Christians and Muslims are almost equal in number and power, Israel is "Jewish," Iraq is half Sunni and half Shī'ī, and both of these are major subdivisions of Islam, while all other Middle East states are "Islamic."

Historical Forces Leading to Modernization

Lebanon's increasing desire for change over the past two centuries has been largely as a result of continuous interaction with Europeans. The Lebanese intellectual elite, equipped with the "new science" of Europe and new world outlooks, has been eager to reassess and, where needed, change the cultural tradition.

Among the leading historical factors promoting modernization in Lebanon have been its confessional structure, the Napoleonic invasion of Egypt, the response of the Ottoman East to growing Western challenges, the opening of missionary educational institutions, and the rise of Western commercial enterprises in the Middle East.

Maronite Interactions with the West

Lebanon's Christian communities, particularly the Maronites, have been in significant interaction with European culture for centuries. In the sixteenth century reforms were initiated in the Maronite Church of Lebanon and a Maronite College was founded in Rome. Since 1736, when the Maronite community reached a concordat with the Pope, its student clergy have received the assistance of the Catholic Church to study in Rome and Padua, where they have learned Latin, Italian, and French, read Catholic thought, and acquainted themselves with the main ideas of the Enlightenment. A number of Maronite scholars have served as librarians in the Vatican.

Trade and cultural relations between the Maronites and France and Italy go back to the seventeenth century, and by the eighteenth century, educated Maronites were serving as conveyors of social and political ideas in Lebanon which were at the roots of the peasants' revolution against the *iqṭā'* (feudal) system in the nineteenth century. Particularly important are the ideas of the priest, Isṭfān al-Dwaihī, Bishop Yūsuf Isṭfān, and Niqūla Murād. The schools they started in Lebanon have had an important effect on the development of education in Lebanon.[1]

Other Christian communities have experienced change as a result of education received in schools opened under the direction of Christian powers in the nineteenth century and enjoyed, therefore, a headstart over non-Christian communities in Lebanon.

The Napoleonic Invasion

Napoleon's invasion of Egypt in 1798 dramatically introduced French liberal thought into the Middle East. Although French slogans of equality, fraternity, and liberty had little appeal to the Egyptian masses, their impact among minorities was long lasting. More than any other single event of that era, the invasion posed a direct challenge to the peoples of the Middle East and revealed the wide cultural chasm between Europeans and Easterners.

8 *Modernization Without Revolution*

The resulting tremors were felt throughout the Eastern Mediterranean. What Napoleon began was continued by his opponent and successor, Muḥammad 'Ali, who relied on European techniques to industrialize the country and improve the efficiency of his army. He used French officers in training his army and employed French technicians in building a new state administration.

The results of Muḥammad 'Ali's modernization policies were carried into Lebanon and Syria from 1832 to 1840 by his lieutenant and son, Ibrāhīm Pasha. Egypt's invasion of Lebanon during this period, in the opinion of some scholars, had the same effect on modernization as Napoleon's invasion had on Egypt's development.[2] While the Egyptian regime in Lebanon, like that of Napoleon in Egypt, fundamentally was resented by the populace, it provided ground for valuable intellectual ferment. Liberal ideas introduced by French and American missions found fertile soil. The peasant revolt against the Egyptians and their ally the amīr Shihāb, overlord of Lebanon, reflected a familiarity with the basic principles of the French Revolution. Equally liberal and modern slogans were used by Ṭānyus Shāhīn, the peasant hero of Kisirwān (a region north of Beirut) in his 1858 revolt against the feudal lords.

Ottoman Reform

A third historical link in the emergence of Lebanese modernization can be traced to the Ottoman period. Lebanon had benefited from the modernizing movement begun in Istanbul since the end of the eighteenth century. Reforms initiated under Sultan Selīm III (1798–1807) and Sultan Maḥmūd II (1808–1839) culminated in two major attempts to lay new constitutional-legal foundations. The first, Hatti-Sharif of Gulhane (1839), issued by Sultan Maḥmūd, was a proclamation emphasizing reform of the polity and its administration. The second, Hatti-Humayun (1856), issued by Sultan 'Abd al-Majīd,[3] proclaimed an end to religious and class discrimination, making public employment open to all subjects "according to their capacity and merit." The prison system was to be reformed and a budget showing yearly revenues and expenditures instituted. Banks and other similar institutions were to be established to "effect a reform in the monetary and financial system," while roads and canals were to be opened to improve communication and increase the wealth of the country. "To accomplish these objects, means shall be sought to profit by the science, the art, and the funds of Europe, and thus gradually to execute them."[4] These reforms left their impact on the administration of the Ottoman provinces of which Lebanon was a part.

New Educational System

A fourth impetus to change has come from the drive for a new educational system, which had been supported by the native clergy since the eighteenth century, and by French, American, Italian, and German missionaries since the early nineteenth century. The rise of foreign schools was abetted by the relatively liberal administration of Ibrāhīm Pasha throughout the 1830s. In 1866 American missionaries founded the Syrian Protestant College, now the American University of Beirut, which introduced into the Arab East liberal education and Western patterns of higher education based on research. A decade later the Jesuits established Saint Joseph University, which today continues to act as a bridge with Europe, particularly France. The impact of these universities on the modernization of Lebanon has been preeminent, as seen below. Graduates of both institutions, especially the former, have found also an intellectual outlet in Egypt. Here, following the British occupation in 1882, they could express through journals and other media the liberal socio-political views that were to influence the cultural development of the entire Arab East, though particularly of Lebanon.[5]

The Mutaṣarrifiyyah Regime

Lebanese society had also experienced social, political, and educational reforms under the mutaṣarrifiyyah regime (1861–1920). This regime came in the wake of two major events: a social revolution in the 1840s, in which Maronite peasants—supported by the clergy—had practically put an end to the feudal structure in Christian Mount Lebanon; and a confessional conflict in the 1860s pitting Christians against Druze and Muslims. European powers interfered and forced the Sultan to introduce a new government, whose governor (*mutaṣarrif*) was to be a Christian, though non-Lebanese, subject of the Sultan and was to be assisted by a council representing the major confessional communities.

The new system introduced peace among the communities, led to a major build-up of schools, roads, and hospitals, and instituted widespread administrative reforms. The prevailing liberal atmosphere under this regime contrasted sharply with the authoritarian regimes in the other parts of the Ottoman Empire. It was under the mutaṣarrifiyyah that the political formula, based on consensus and conciliation, was put to test and proved successful.

The mutaṣarrifiyyah regime in Lebanon lasted from 1861 to 1920. Although the Ottomans abolished the mutaṣarrifiyyah in 1914 and appointed a military governor to handle Ottoman military affairs in the region, the mutaṣarrifiyyah administrative system continued undisturbed throughout the war. The French made no serious administrative changes following their 1918 occupation until 1920 when they declared a State of Greater Lebanon. This in effect abolished the mutaṣarrifiyyah regime and expanded Lebanon's frontiers by adding new territories that were not part of the previous regime.

The Mandate Period

The frontiers of the State of Greater Lebanon were those of Lebanon as it now exists, while the name was changed early during the Mandate to State of Lebanon.

As used here, the French Mandate is taken to cover the period 1920–1943. It may be argued that the Mandate was not legally ended until 1945, when the United Nations assumed the legal obligations of the League of Nations and Lebanon joined that body as a sovereign, independent state. Actually, evacuation of French military forces from Lebanon was completed in 1946. However, the Lebanese consider 1943 to mark the end of the Mandate, since it was in that year that the Lebanese Parliament amended the 1926 Constitution, abrogated all articles referring to mandatory status, and declared Lebanon's total independence.

Prior to the Mandate's beginning in 1920, competition among the Great Powers to control the diverse confessions was a conspicuous influence in Lebanon. France protected the Maronites, Russia the Greek Orthodox, and Britain the tiny Protestant groupings, Jews, and the Druze. France's imperial control of Lebanon during the Mandate helped modernize Lebanese administration and gave the country a national constitutional framework. French high commissioners, high-ranking civil servants, and consultants were to transform Lebanon between 1920 and 1943 in the light of a "*mission civilisatrice.*"

Under the Mandate, Lebanon had also acquired a parliament elected by popular vote, a president elected by the parliament, a council of ministers, an independent judiciary, and a modern fiscal system. By the time the Mandate ended in 1943, the Lebanese—particularly the inhabitants of Beirut and of Mount Lebanon—had experienced a large measure also of social Westernization. The hat replaced the *fez;* trousers replaced the traditional baggy pants; white shirts displaced the *qamīs;* the necktie, the pen, and the watch emerged as symbols of modernity; and French language, music, literature, and style of living crowded out their Arabic counterparts in the life of the upper classes. As is always the case in such processes of acculturation, the upper classes were the first to be affected, with the low-income classes changing timidly and belatedly.

Post-Independence Factors

While our analysis deals mainly with government, a major finding below is that precisely the limited role of government has been a positive factor prompting modernization in the past, by permitting the private sector and entrepreneurial incentives to develop unhindered. Modernization also has been encouraged by such coordinated forces as the radical elite, communications media, foreign consultants, and business enterprise itself.

Attitudes of Political Leaders

Most of Lebanon's top government leaders have studied in French schools, whether in Lebanon or in France, where their political ideas and nationalist ideologies have been moulded, along with administrative skills, in a context of extensive legal education. For them, modernization has been conceived more or less legalistically; they envisage reform of administration, society, and state as a process to be achieved through law.

In parliament, elaborate official statements in support of modernization have been delivered by premiers seeking votes of confidence of newly formed cabinets. The first such statement after independence was delivered by Premier Riyāḍ al-Ṣulḥ in 1943 and it emphasized national unity and loyalty as superior politically to confessional, regional, and feudal loyalties.[6]

Lebanese cabinets generally have committed themselves to administrative reforms; proclaimed the right of all citizens to equality, freedom, and economic security; encouraged the development of a professional civil service; and emphasized the significance of a broadly based responsible citizenry. While governmental commitment to modernization is basically formal and lacks sustained momentum, the Lebanese government has presented over the past decade extensive reform objectives.

Interspersed throughout the political structure, both in the center and in local areas, are the zaʿīms. Lebanon's decision-making processes can not be understood or analyzed without major allowance for this element. The zaʿīms are leaders with almost charismatic power over their followers, revered and depended upon for services of all sorts. The more underdeveloped the region the more likely it is to give rise to zaʿīms. The zaʿīm usually owes his position to a family which enjoyed leadership status for centuries (e.g. the Arslāns, Junblāts) or to his individual ability as a manipulator of men (e.g., Shamʿūn). In the eyes of his followers, the zaʿīm is so firmly established (either because of what he represents as a scion of a great family—e.g., Junblāt —or because of his former achievements, or because of his personality) that he is generally supported by his constituency irrespective of his political stands or his successes or failures as a legislator.

The term "political formula," as used throughout this study, refers to the rules that have been agreed upon by Lebanese leaders since independence in 1943 on how the country is to be governed. This is a composite of written laws and unwritten agreements and practices, comprising traditional norms set by the consensus of the za'īms on major policy matters, constitutional stipulations, and allocation of offices by confessions.

Radical Elite

More than government, the radical elite urge rapid and extensive modernization and blame government leaders for lukewarm commitment to modernization. This group consists primarily of intellectuals who are not in power. Some teach in universities and high schools or work as journalists, but most are either unemployed or employed in jobs which do not satisfy them materially and intellectually. These tend to join leftist or rightist organizations, congregate around a dissenting political leader, or publish usually short-lived journals and newspapers. They include communists, socialists, pan-Syrian and pan-Arab nationalists. Radical elites meet in university centers, coffee houses, restaurants, and hotel lobbies and heatedly debate current political issues. Through pamphlets and articles they exert continuing pressure on the "system" to speed reform.

The concerns of the radical elite tend to be political primarily, then social, and next economic. Politically they seek to bring more efficient unity into the Arab world and to introduce revolutionary government. Socially they seek a restructuring of society along ideological lines. Economically they tend to follow Marxist lines. Although economic concerns may at times gain precedence over social ones, rarely does either dominate political issues, for it is through political action that the Lebanese radical expects to effect and accelerate change or promote modernization. Only a new ruling class, they contend, with no vested interests and an outlook truly representative of the people can be expected to introduce extensive reforms and bring the benefits of modernization to the mass strata of society. Radicals often disagree on policy matters and lack sufficient organization across party lines to pose a serious danger to the prevailing political order. However, their negative role as critics of the governing class has spurred reform and will probably continue to do so even if, as seems likely, they themselves fail to assume power. It was socialist pressure, for example, that led to the law requiring politicians and bureaucrats to disclose their wealth and to submit to judicial scrutiny if suspected of illegal accumulation of wealth.

Communications Media

A major instrument in the spreading of modernization in Lebanon has been the communications media. The printing press was introduced in the eighteenth century by Maronite clergy and its use expanded in the nineteenth century by American missionaries and Jesuits. Beirut today is a regional publishing center for the rest of the Arab world, publishing 49 political newspapers daily;[7] 48 political journals and 133 non-political magazines weekly; and 4 political magazines and 140 non-political magazines monthly. In terms of newspaper circulation, Lebanon ranked among the upper third of about 125 countries in 1959.[8] Although it is difficult to determine the present extent of newspaper circulation, the French language newspaper *L'Orient* and the Arabic *al-Nahār*, printing daily about 25,000 copies each, probably have the widest circulation. Other dailies have about 8,000, with a few others reaching as high as 1,000 and some as little as a few hundred. Some weeklies, such as *al-Usbū' al-'Arabi*, have a circulation of about 30,000.

Moreover, for every paper sold there are about five readers. Like Palermo in the Middle Ages transmitting Arabic thought to Europe, Beirut has become a transmitter of Western thought to the Arabs. It is a center of translation, commentary, and the sale of Western works. The liberal political atmosphere prevailing in the country is largely responsible for the rapid expansion of communications media since the mid-1940s. These, despite their shortcomings, have remained free and daring sources of criticism as well as consistent proponents of modernization.

The newer media of radio, television, and cinema have greatly extended perspectives and desires of Lebanese citizens.[9] Undoubtedly, the influence of the cinema on cultural patterns also has been substantial. External aspects such as dress and housing are—as well as attitudes and beliefs—evidence of change.

Foreign Consultants

Foreign consultants have been a highly visible agent of change. With few extreme nationalists and with a long tradition of dealing with foreigners, Lebanon has often called on advanced nations and international organizations for technical advice. Dozens of experts from the United States, Britain, France, Belgium, and Holland have studied, reported, and made recommendations about an extensive spectrum of modernization-related items, postal administration, statistical data processing, financial administration, the tax structure, police administration, and human resource development programs.[10] With the exception of the extremely significant IRFED[11] project (see below) most consultations have been based on short periods of observation. Although this has minimized effective implementation, it is important to observe that no major development project has been undertaken without recourse to foreign consultants.

Business Enterprises

Business firms as agents of change deserve special notice. History and physical location, together with extensive cultural connections with the West and the Middle East, have made Lebanon a major trading and exchange center in the region. In 1967 the Beirut Chamber of Commerce and Industry listed 6,380 registered business firms in the country, including major banks, insurance companies, airlines, oil companies, and chemical industries. Lebanese, Syrian, Saudi, Kuwaiti, and Western entrepreneurs in Beirut provide the city with the experience of some of the region's finest business innovators, who often have had extensive dealings in Europe, Latin America, the United States, Africa, and the oil-rich countries of the Middle East.[12]

Foreign firms, in training nationals in management techniques, often serve as "multipliers," as new firms become established by the foreign-trained employees.

The forces referred to above have not been the only ones working for modernization, nor have they operated totally in the same direction. Indeed, factors opposing modernization can be identified in all of the above-mentioned forces. Nevertheless their net effect has been both obvious and marked, while being moderated by the existing plural, communal, and liberal Lebanese socio-economic structure. This structure is the subject of the following chapter.

II
The Communal Society—Modernization under Laissez-Faire

The present chapter deals with land and climate, population, education, and economic tendencies as factors affecting the modernization process in Lebanon.

Land and Climate

Lebanon's temperate climate and favorable location have been positive factors in its development. The Mediterranean has served as the highway for inhabitants of the Lebanese shore over several millennia, bringing them in contact with other civilizations and providing them with continuing stimulants for change. Typically Mediterranean, the climate is temperate with clear-cut seasonal variations: rainfall is plentiful between November and March, assuring a lush spring and giving way to a rain-free summer. Winter rain and snow account for hundreds of springs, a dozen tiny, picturesque rivers, and cedar, pine, and oak forests. History has been less kind than nature to these forests; since forests were rare in the arid Middle East, the Lebanese forests were gradually depleted to build temples, towns, and navies for the succession of conquerors who ruled over the strategic Fertile Crescent. Depletion was so severe that remaining forests in Lebanon cover only a bare seven percent of its surface.

From aesthetic and touristic points of view, Lebanon is fortunate in its seashore and mountains. The seashore harbors the historic cities of Tyre (Ṣūr), Sidon (Ṣaida), Beirut, Junieh, Byblos (Jbail), and Tripoli (Ṭarāblus). The sand and rock beaches, harbors, and yacht clubs provide recreation for the emerging bourgeois class and an added source of income for the poorer classes who inhabit the seashore towns and villages.

Shielding the country from its desert-like interior, two chains of mountains, Mount Lebanon and the Anti-Lebanon, provide a haven for minority groups who once felt threatened by the dominant religious orthodoxies—both Christian and Muslim—of the Middle East. The Anti-Lebanon range of mountains is relatively poor and barren; unlike Mount Lebanon it has not had the economic benefits of tourism or of educational facilities. Mount Lebanon, beginning just a few kilometers from the seashore, rises to altitudes up to 10,000 feet. Its hills and peaks, from the southern part of the country to the "Cedars of Lebanon" in the north, contain hundreds of villages, many of which, especially in the vicinity of Beirut, have become major tourist centers. This shore 1-1 mountain combination can accommodate, in the appropriate season, both skier and swimmer.

Unlike Syria, Iraq, and Egypt, Lebanon has no extensive plains and no river remotely comparable to the Tigris, Euphrates, or Nile. Its plains seem more like "interruptions" of the rugged mountain chains that cover 70 percent of the country, the remaining 30 percent being agricultural land, of which the most fertile is the Biqā' Plain. About 25 percent of the land under cultivation is irrigated—not a poor ratio by Middle Eastern standards, but still inadequate. Partially because of the hardships imposed on them by the rugged terrain, peasants have emigrated abroad or to the city and have "educated" their children "so that they will never have to till the soil again."

Lebanon has no oil resources, though it possesses two refineries—one in Tripoli and the other in Sidon—which process oil piped from Iraq and Saudi Arabia respectively. Industrial minerals are meager in quantity and poor in quality. A small quantity of iron ore is being mined in the Metn district and in the districts of Batrūn and Byblos north of Beirut. Salt is still produced in the traditional manner in the coastal towns north of Byblos, but stone quarrying has accommodated itself to modern technology and diverse architectural needs, supplying builders with ornamental marble, onyx, and limestone.

Lebanon's location on the eastern Mediterranean ensured its contacts with Europe, which, since the Renaissance, have stimulated modernization on a world-wide scale. Location and climate have given added inducements to missionaries and foreign entrepreneurs to visit the country, establish institutions, and propagate their missions. To this extent a commodious climate and strategic location have served as positive factors in the process of social change.

Population

Since obtaining independence Lebanon has preferred not to conduct a population census, owing to the fear that the results might strain the political formula by which it is governed. The last census of the Lebanese population, conducted in 1932 under the French Mandate, showed a total population of 793,426 with a Christian majority in the ratio of 6 to 5. This has been the basis of the political formula for assigning political and administrative offices for nearly four decades.[1] Since 1932 population estimates and projections have had to be made on the basis of administrative records and studies by foreign consultants.[2] Table 2.1 provides a comparative guide to Lebanon's population relative to other Middle-East areas, based on recent available estimates according to the United Nations.[3]

If non-Arab residents, Palestinian refugees, and unregistered Syrian workers and residents are included, the 1969 population of Lebanon approximated the three million mark.[4] With an area of 10,400 km^2,[5] Lebanon is one of the smallest countries in the Middle East, about half the size of Israel (pre-1967). It is by far the most densely populated, with 268 persons per square kilometer as compared with a general Middle-Eastern-Mediterranean average of about 30 per square kilometer.[6]

The IRFED estimates of age distribution for the late 1950s show that the population of Lebanon, like the rest of the region, is young, with approximately 50 percent of the people below 20

TABLE 2.1
1970 Population, 1963–1970 Growth Rate, Area, and Density of Eight Middle East Countries

Country	Population (1,000s)	Area sq. km. (1,000s)	Annual Percent of Increase 1963–1970	Density
Iraq	9,440	434.9	3.2	22
Israel	2,889	20.7	2.8	140
Jordan*	2,317	97.7	3.7	24
Kuwait	711	16.0	9.0	44
Lebanon**	2,787	10.4	2.9	268
Saudi Arabia	7,740	2,149.7	2.7	4
Syria	6,098	185.2	3.0	33
United Arab Republic	33,329	1,001.4	2.5	33

*Including registered Palestinian refugees.
**Excluding registered Palestinian refugees, numbering 175,958 on June 30, 1970.
Source: United Nations, *Demographic Yearbook*, 1970.

years of age. Such a ratio, arising out of the region's high fertility, tends to pose severe handicaps on development by inhibiting savings and by raising consumption needs in both the private and public (including educational) sectors.

By Asian and Middle Eastern standards the Lebanese population is comparatively healthy and life expectancy relatively high. The per capita calorie intake of 2,540 in 1966 is one of the highest in the Arab World. It compares favorably with those of other Arab countries. Starvation is practically unknown, and all major diseases have been brought under control. Past scourges such as smallpox and cholera have become rare.[7] Better housing and education and more extensive medical services have helped to reduce greatly many diseases and infant deaths. Using the number of inhabitants per physician as an index of modernization, Lebanon has ranked well above the world median in recent years.[8]

There are 150 hospitals in Lebanon, having a total bed capacity of 9,000. These hospitals are supported by government and philanthropic organizations or are privately owned, and in Beirut at least six of these are considered to provide high-quality care, including the new thirty million dollar Medical Center of the American University of Beirut, which may well serve as a model hospital and research center for the entire Middle East. Private hospitals accommodate about 60 percent of the patients and government hospitals the rest.[9]

Childbirth among the poor continues to be high. This is particularly true among rural people who tend to think of children as Allah's gift, and therefore beyond the manipulation of man's free will. Among the middle and upper classes, irrespective of religion, birth control methods have been accepted with little or no opposition—religious, ethical, or social. A family of three or four is considered to be a correct norm. The quiet acceptance of birth control by the highly secularized upper classes is partially due to the fact that birth control never became a public issue and was never subjected to heated debate, as it was in Italy and the United States. This may be due to the diversity of religions and confessions, as well as to the dominance of political and religious considerations in Lebanon.[10] The privileged position of the boy baby over the girl baby is still maintained, although the line of discrimination between the sexes is being blurred. A sign of the privileged position of the boy is the attempt of parents who have a number of daughters to continue to "try for a boy," while practically no such attempt is made if the situation is reversed. Monogamy is generally the rule. While in Islam polygamy is allowed it is rapidly dying out as an institution, not only in Lebanon, but throughout the world of Islam. Only a negligible minority among the Muslim Lebanese are still polygamous.

The traditional supremacy of the male is still observed, especially in ceremonial functions. The father is still served, obeyed, and in a way feared by the wife—but again profound changes are shaking the pedestal of male supremacy. The Middle Eastern female has always played a strong role "behind closed doors" in the management of the household and continues to do so, particularly among the lower income groups.

Confessional Groupings

The rugged and highly diversified topography of Lebanon is perhaps the reason behind Lebanon's heterogeneous communal structure. For centuries, religious minorities in the Middle East sought refuge in the mountains of Lebanon, where they developed, with a minimum of interference, autonomous confessional structures within the universal Islamic state—Umayyad, 'Abbāsid, or Ottoman.[11] Its entire decision-making process is conditioned by its religious composition.[12] The Muslim communities consist of the Sunnis (46 percent) Shī'īs (40 percent) and Druze (14 percent), while the Christian communities consist of Maronites, Greek Orthodox, Greek Catholics, Syrian Orthodox, Syrian Catholics, Assyrian and Chaldean Catholics, Armenians, and diverse Protestant groupings. There are also some Jews and a miscellaneous category of other small confessional groupings.

Of these communities the largest and the most influential are the Maronites and Sunnis. The Maronite Christians, who trace their origin to Saint Mārūn of the fifth century, are now members of the Roman Catholic church and intellectually and culturally oriented toward France. The Sunni Lebanese identify with the larger Sunni community, which is the predominant community in the Arab world.[13] The Shī'īs are a dissident religious group within Islam; although religiously distinct from the Sunnis, they tend to join hands with them when major political issues are at stake. The Druze developed from Shī'ī Islam in the eleventh century and are a doctrinally separate grouping; however, they maintain strong links with Islam.[14] The Druze and the Greek Orthodox frequently fill an important mediatory role between the Sunnis and Maronites.

Each confessional grouping tends to dominate a single specific region. The Sunnis dominate the coastal towns and are about equal in number with the Christians in Beirut. The Maronites dominate Mount Lebanon, the hills in the vicinity of Beirut, and the mountains in the north up to the Cedars. The Greek Orthodox are found in the Kūrah district near Tripoli and in Beirut. The Druze occupy the hills south of Beirut.[15]

The latest groups to come to Lebanon have been the Armenian and Palestinian refugees. The former are found mostly in Beirut; the latter are still largely in camps throughout Lebanon and in the suburbs of Beirut. Armenian migration into Lebanon first began in the wake of the 1895-96 "Turkish massacre" and continued after World War I as a result of Ataturk's "Turkifying" policy. In 1924 the French Mandatory regime in Lebanon gave Lebanese citizenship to the Armenian refugees. The latest Armenian migration took place in the late 1930s after Turkish annexation of the Sanjaq of Alexandretta. At the end of World War II a small number left Lebanon for Soviet Armenia. Armenian refugees were given land in the Biqā' plateau, where they founded the village of 'Anjar, but the majority live in Beirut and its suburbs. There are about 100,000 Armenians in Lebanon, recognized by law as two religious communities: "Orthodox" and "Catholic." The Armenian community is active in Lebanese politics, with the Dashnaqs, their most important political party, working closely with the Lebanese Katā'ib party. They favor the continuation of the confessional system, which assures them of legitimate access to power.

The Palestinian refugees are not a legally recognized community, and therefore are not, unlike the other communities, entitled to proportionate representation in political and bureaucratic offices. The Palestinian refugees entered Lebanon in 1947-48 as a result of the conflicts leading to the establishment of the state of Israel. Lebanon, like the rest of the Arab countries, does not recognize the state of Israel and does not accept the finality of refugee status for the Palestinians living within its borders. This is the reason why Palestinians have not been given citizenship and why they have not asked for it. The diversity of Lebanon's communal structure has led scholars to use terms such as "museum," "mosaic," "plural," "communal," "multiple" in describing the country.[16]

In the past, the autonomy of the various communities was legitimized and organized by the Ottoman *millet* system. Independence brought the communities together politically, but left to each the power to administer laws of personal status, manage its religious courts, and operate its confessional school systems.

The communities have behaved as national groupings and have manifested characteristics of inner solidarity. The situation in this respect resembles Apter's description of ethnic formation as another form of nationhood. The primary attachment of many in new nations is not to the polity of the modern state but to the polity of the ethnic group. Such ethnic attachments do not wither away with the formation of a national state.[17]

Communal groupings in Lebanon have demonstrated great elasticity and determination to survive. In business and political dealings members of the same confession tend to work together, treat each other deferentially, and establish bargaining positions with respect to other confessions. Links between them and the political process are clearly stronger than links with political or other voluntary associations. Indeed, such associations have often had to adjust to the confessional contours of the "Lebanese mosaic," often to the detriment of their own declared objectives. For example the Katā'ib party, while stating that it is nonconfessional, in fact is essentially Maronite. The Najjadah Party similarly claims to be nonconfessional but in fact is almost exclusively Sunni Muslim in membership. When major political issues are at stake the group tends to formulate its position on the basis of its religion rather than on the basis of economic or social standings.[18]

Confessional loyalties reached their height during the period leading up to the Lebanese civil conflict of 1958. At the time the incumbent president, Kamīl Sham'ūn, adhered to the Eisenhower Doctrine and seemed to lean extensively toward the Western camp and the Baghdad Pact countries. In thus seemingly violating the policy of neutrality established by the National Pact, he was bitterly opposed by nationalist and leftist leaders, mostly Muslims, who looked to President Nasser (Nāṣir) of Egypt for leadership. The resulting civil strife assumed, in part, a confessional character, with perhaps a majority of the Christians siding with Shamʿūn and a clear majority of the Muslims in opposition to his policy. The army, led by an aspirant for the presidency, Fuʾād Shihāb, refused to suppress the uprising and agreed merely to preserve order and keep the combatants apart. The ensuing civil conflict, which developed into continuous skirmishes between Shamʿūn and opposition groupings, ended by the election of General Shihāb as president in 1958. Since then Lebanon has retained a policy of neutrality without in any way curtailing its long standing ties with Western countries. The arms purchase negotiated by the Lebanese government early in 1972 with Western democratic as well as with socialist countries is an indication of Lebanon's attempt at maintaining its neutrality. Confessional loyalties were again clearly discernible in the cabinet crisis of 1969, which arose as a result of the operation of Palestinian commandos against Israel from within Lebanese frontiers. Although such loyalties are undergoing changes due to migration patterns, new job opportunities, and education, these factors have not been sufficient to alter the primary role of the religious community as a socio-political entity.

Emigration

The Lebanese, more than any other Arab people, are dispersed throughout all regions of the world. About two million

Lebanese citizens reside in foreign lands, constituting a diaspora of direct importance to the modernization of Lebanon. One-third of these live in the United States; a little more than one-third live in Latin America, principally Brazil and Argentina; the remainder are distributed throughout Africa, Europe, the oil-producing countries of the Middle East, Australia, and New Zealand.

Emigration to the United States has been slowed since the 1920s as a result of strict immigration policies. Similarly, emigration to Africa declined rapidly in the 1950s owing to the rise of nationalist regimes in that region's newly independent states; generally such regimes have been suspicious of immigrants, preferring to have their resources developed by nationals. Emigration to Saudi Arabia, Kuwait, and Libya is usually of a temporary nature. Almost all such emigrants return to Lebanon after they have accumulated enough capital to start them off in a business venture at home.

The reasons for emigration have been various: some have wanted to escape confessional conflicts, some to avoid working the barren mountain slopes, and others, as education broadened their vision, have seen better opportunities for raising families in lands beyond the seas. The New World has provided the Lebanese with opportunities to engage in work they would not have undertaken at home. Status, face-saving considerations, and modes of life prevailing in Lebanon have rendered it difficult for the average Lebanese to indulge freely in menial work. Yet in foreign climes he has been ready to do any job without the fear of cultural constraints. He has been able to live simply in his adopted country and year after year save money until he has accumulated enough to invest in, or return to, his old country.

The fact that most emigrants are Christian and Druze is

largely due to their religious minority status. Muslims tend to find security in being members of the dominant community of the Middle East, and to prefer it to a minority status in a foreign land.[19] This point is further corroborated by patterns of emigration from Syria, Jordan, and Egypt. The emigrants constitute a far-reaching network—one as extensive, if not as intensive, as that of the Jewish Diaspora—that lends political, economic, and cultural support to Lebanon. Remittances from emigrants help finance the education of many poor villagers and sponsor the establishment of schools, libraries, and charitable organizations. The wealthier among those who return often invest in business, industry, or modern farming, another significant contribution to development and modernization. About 50,000 original emigrants are estimated to have returned between 1944 and 1962.

An important result of Lebanese emigration has been to loosen class immobility. Poor families living as clients of rich landlords have been able, using funds obtained from relatives abroad, to purchase land from the landlords, send their sons to school, and undertake business ventures. Similarly, emigrants returning rich, who were poor prior to emigration, have been able to challenge the established families in their region and in the process introduce important changes in the social order.[20]

Rural-Urban Distribution and Comparisons

An extremely important process of social change, one by no means unique to Lebanon, has been the growing migration from village to city. About 60 percent of the Lebanese live in villages or towns having populations varying from a few hundred to as many as 10 to 15 thousand.[21] In the past, the village, tribe, or farm was the principal unit of habitation. In its present-day form, a typical village consists of some 500 houses, built close together around a church or a mosque,[22] with the village land lying around it all and most inhabitants engaged in agriculture.

Generally the village is of one faith, though in a number of cases there may be a dominant rather than exclusive religion. Rarely is there a more or less even division in terms of religious affiliation.[23] The village is administered internally by a municipal council, while its relations with the central government in such matters as registration of births, deaths, and testimonies are conducted through an elected *mukhtar* (mayor). A type of solidarity in relation to other villages exists and affects social and economic relations in a manner similar to that of confessional solidarity. Until recently the village tended to be a highly cohesive socio-political unit.[24] Villagers tend to dress alike throughout a region but have distinct colloquial usages that immediately identify their local place of residence. Except in rare cases, villagers own their homes and enough land to guarantee them basic subsistence. Until the automobile and radio broke down the village walls, the village was self-sufficient. People were born, raised, married, and buried within its confines and stories are still told of villagers who never travelled farther than ten kilometers from their native place.

This cohesiveness is being eroded by urban emigration patterns and by changes in employment and social structure patterns. Modernization is changing the life-style and the class structure of the village; it has brought new wealth, houses, facilities, consumer tastes, and even a commuter-type economy. No village in Lebanon is more than a one-hour drive from a city or more than a two-hour drive from Beirut. Modernization of the village began under the impetus of schools and emigrants and is proceeding under additional influences such as mass media, cars, and buses. The rise of prosperous urban centers has led to moves by the poor and rich alike.[25] On the whole, the Christian village has experienced greater modernization than the Muslim village, because of earlier exposure to modern schooling and emigration, and also perhaps to differing attitudes toward change.[26]

Climate, topography, and the smallness of the country have also influenced movements of population. In the summer many city dwellers take refuge in the mountain villages; in winter many villages are drained of half their population as residents move to a warmer and more comfortable city. In other cases, villagers may move almost *en masse* to undertake seasonal work in other villages. Here again confessional considerations tend to prevail, with Muslims preferring villages in the mountains inhabited by their co-religionists, and Christians tending to seek out Christian villages.[27]

While there are 2,200 villages scattered throughout the country, there are only two major cities, Beirut and Tripoli, and a few towns—Byblos, Sidon, Tyre, Zaḥlah, and Ba'albek.[28] Beirut stands out as obviously the most modernized urban center in Lebanon. Tripoli, a predominantly Muslim city, is receiving special governmental attention to raise it to the level of Beirut. An international fair is being built which may take from one to four more years to complete, depending on the yearly allocation of funds. New hotels, restaurants, and a major highway to Beirut are expected to ensure a steady flow of tourists.[29] Beirut, with a population of about 800,000, and Tripoli, with 200,000, account for about a third of the entire population, giving Lebanon a much higher percentage (40) of urban population than is the average for the less developed regions.[30] Both developed rapidly during World War II and Beirut in particular has continued to grow largely as a result of the oil and commercial boom in the Arabian peninsula. Foreign communities have grown as a result of discovery of oil and the expansion of American-European markets in the Middle East. These communities are involved in education, church, and business activities throughout the Middle East.

Migration from villages to towns and cities is growing steadily with the growth of services and industrial investments in the urban centers, particularly Beirut and Tripoli. Relatives descend on relatives and friends on friends; those without either usually camp in the first empty space that seems available. Thousands of squatters on government-owned land constitute a problem, refusing to evacuate land they now consider to be theirs. Often squatters have the support of one or more za'īms, and have succeeded, so far, in obviating government measures taken against them. An estimated 8,000 families in Beirut live in shacks made of cardboard, tin, used wood, or canvas. In each family one or more members is employed. Although beggars have almost disappeared from the streets, their place seems to have been taken by a younger generation (5 to 15 years of age) who pursue analogous marginal trades such as selling chewing gum or wiping car windows.

In spite of the push from the village and the pull by the city, there is not, as yet, a discernible shortage in housing; Beirut has many vacant apartment buildings whose landlords would rather keep an apartment vacant than rent it at a low price. Many oil-rich, non-Lebanese landlords have purchased luxury buildings in Beirut as security and not necessarily as a source of added income. Often a part of such buildings is reserved for the landlord or his family for occasional sojourns in Beirut. Keeping the apartments unrented makes the building easier to sell, a factor of considerable importance, since Lebanese law protects the tenant in many ways. Once a rental contract is made it is extremely difficult for the landlord to raise the rent or evict a paying tenant. For these reasons a landlord must carefully consider the amount of rent and the type of tenant if future legal difficulties are to be avoided.

Rent is relatively high and trade unions have been pressing the government to build low-cost housing.[31] Yet the government's 1965 decision to undertake housing projects for the poor has met a great deal of skepticism, even by the poor, since housing has been an exclusively private concern; even the government rents most of its buildings from private landlords. The skepticism has been justified. So far, attempts to start projects have ended in failure with some abandoned for lack of funds or by diversions of funds to other projects.

The major Lebanese cities, like most modern ones elsewhere, face rapid development requiring new technical skills and organizational capabilities.[32] Such resources are rare and their build-up is slow, tedious, and unassured. Generally speaking Beirut has a modern mechanism for every service it performs, yet somehow the historical character of the city determines actual performance. For example, garbage is collected by the latest-model garbage truck. Before it reaches the truck, however, the garbage has been piled on street corners and occasionally strewn in the streets by children, animals, rain, or wind.

Education

Modernization of Lebanon under a laissez-faire economic system has also been promoted by the communal basis of education. The heterogeneity provided by the Lebanese sects led to competition among foreign Christian missionaries to establish schools having a modernizing orientation. On the whole, the school system continues to be a reflection of Lebanese diverse confessional structure. While such diversity may hamper some goals and prerequisites of modernization, it has supported pluralism, multi-linguistic training, and easy access to high-quality education on the part of limited-income families who have made the right connections.

The institutions of higher education in Lebanon are largely the product of foreign missionary or cultural activity. Only very few of these higher institutions are fully Lebanese. They include a dozen universities, colleges, and institutes, all located in Beirut or its immediate environs; they fall into four categories —American, French, national, and national-foreign.[33] The main American institutions are the American University of Beirut and the Beirut College for Women. The French institutions are Saint Joseph University and three entities with which it is closely associated, a School of Letters, a Center of Higher Mathematical Studies, and an Institute of Middle-East Geography. The national institutions are the Lebanese University and the Lebanese Academy of Fine Arts. The national-foreign institutions are the Hagazian College and the Arab University.[34]

American Institutions

The American University of Beirut, with an enrollment of about 4,000 students, is the largest private American university outside of the United States.[35] It consists of four faculties: Arts and Sciences, Medical Sciences (Medicine, Pharmacy, Public Health, and Nursing), Engineering and Architecture, and Agriculture, the first containing the best departments in Lebanon offering a modern social-science program leading to the Master of Arts degree. Enrollment essentially is set by the University's Board of Trustees and is not likely to be augmented despite increasing numbers of applications.

Graduates in economics, sociology, public administration, political science, and business administration tend to occupy key positions in Lebanese business and banking, partly as a result of the extensive commercial interest of American firms in Lebanon and the Middle East. They also hold a number of key posts in the bureaucracy—particularly in the Ministries of Foreign Affairs, Finance, Economy, and Social Affairs—though the bureaucracy is dominated by the graduates of Saint Joseph. More recently the Ministry of General Planning, Central Bank, and Civil Service Council have further tapped the research capability of the faculty, especially economists. A number of departments in the Faculty of Arts and Sciences offer programs leading to the Ph.D.[36]

The Faculty of Medicine runs the most advanced medical center in the Arab world and graduates a core of Lebanese physicians who have pioneered in medical work throughout the Middle East. The Ministry of Public Health maintains contacts with this faculty and draws on its physicians for consultation. The newly built medical center is engaged in extensive research programs aimed at strengthening the field of preventive medicine in Lebanon and the Middle East.

The young faculties of Engineering and Architecture and of Agriculture have established linkages with state ministries and cooperate with them in town planning, traffic control, agricultural research, and agricultural training.

The Beirut College for Women (all other university-level institutions are coeducational), founded in 1926 by American missionaries, enrolls about 600 girls in a four-year program leading to a Bachelor's degree in the liberal arts. It has a faculty of about 60, of whom less than one-third are Americans. The program is modelled after American liberal-arts colleges, offering also a two-year course in commerce. The college maintains close relations with the American University of Beirut and draws on the latter's extensive library and faculty resources.

These American educational institutions are essentially regional, serving not only Lebanon but the entire Middle East and beyond. This is particularly true of the American University of Beirut and, to a lesser degree, of all the other American institutions, including those at the elementary and secondary levels.

French Institutions

Saint Joseph University, founded in 1881 as part of a Jesuit missionary drive, has evolved into a full-fledged academic center, and has continued to maintain its Jesuit character. Unlike the American University of Beirut, it primarily serves Lebanon, particularly the Catholic Maronite community, rather than the whole region.[37] Its main strength lies in its law school and humanities programs. Its law school continues to be the most influential school in the country, supplying most of the top personnel of the political system and of the national bureaucracy. Equally important has been its influence on the Lebanese University, which is developing largely in line with the Saint Joseph model.

Saint Joseph has excellent medical and engineering faculties and currently operates the only school of dentistry in Lebanon.[38] The prestigious Catholic Press operates under its auspices, as does the Oriental Institute, with its excellent library and research facilities.

National Institution

When the Lebanese University was founded by the government as a national institution in 1953, it consisted of a Higher

Teachers Training College and a Statistics Institute, to which faculties of Law, Arts (Letters), and Sciences were added in 1959. In 1961 an Institute of Social Science was established, in 1966 a Faculty of Fine Arts, and in 1967 a Faculty of Journalism. Like other Arab national universities it enjoys administrative autonomy, though its full-time professors are considered members of the civil service and it operates under the general supervision of the Ministry of Education. Enrollment for 1968–69 was about 10,000, of whom about one-fourth were members of the bureaucracy seeking advancement through a university degree. The fact that its faculty and student body (like those of Saint Joseph University and the Arab University) are largely on a part-time basis tends to reduce its effectiveness and academic quality. Its library and laboratory facilities are still in their infancy, while a number of operational characteristics—lecture-type classes, use of the so-called *cours* (typed lectures of the professor sold as books), and exclusive reliance on a final examination—have been criticized by students and young professors as being antiquated.

National-Foreign Institutions

Hagazian College, founded in 1955, is a liberal-arts college supported by the Armenian communities in Beirut and the United States. Its program is modelled on the American system and it tries to maintain close relations with the American University of Beirut. The language of instruction in its arts and sciences program is English. The student body is primarily Armenian and is expanding at a greater pace than the college's facilities can accommodate.

Arab University, with faculties of arts, commerce, and law, was founded by the Muslim Philanthropic and Benevolent Society of Beirut in cooperation with the University of Alexandria in Egypt. Since opening in 1960, its enrollment reached over 14,000 in 1968–69. It is primarily financed by the Egyptian government with its degrees awarded by the University of Alexandria; top teaching and administrative staff are Egyptian.

The Ministry of Education estimates the total number of students in higher education (those beyond the regular high-school level baccalaureate program) for 1968–69 to be very nearly 32,376, of whom only 13,637 were Lebanese.[39] This ratio of non-Lebanese to Lebanese students has significant cultural and political implications: on the one hand it shows Lebanon's influence on the Arab East through education of potential leaders in all fields; on the other hand the presence of a large number of non-Lebanese students, who feel differently about major political issues in the area, causes conflicts that can disturb the delicately balanced communal structure. Few countries have similar foreign-domestic student ratios and corresponding educational responsibilities to the regions they service.

Certain characteristics are shared by Lebanese educational institutions: first, the most advanced and still the most influential universities in Lebanon are private and foreign; hence, largely outside the influence of the Ministry of Education. Second, the language of instruction of the most established universities and colleges is not the native Arabic, but either French or English. This has profound implications in both the long-run missions and day-to-day relations—cultural, political, administrative, commercial—of these institutions. Third, the curricula of all the foreign institutions were not originally conceived with Lebanese national development aims in mind. This is also true of the national institutions, which, in miming their foreign counterparts, have analogous curricula. There is, for example, excessive emphasis on law, literature, and commerce at the expense of scientific, professional, and technological training.

Pre-university education, like higher education, is very much governed by the communal nature of Lebanese society. Although there is one uniform prerequisite for entrance into a university or a government job (a Baccalaureate certificate), the pre-university system has an atomistic structure. The communities of Lebanon have always jealously guarded their right to operate their respective confessional schools.[40] The result has been a dazzling mosaic of schools and programs conforming in erratically varying degrees to the government baccalaureate program. There are numerous non-government schools operated by charitable organizations, missionaries, enterprising individuals, and foreign communities. Some, such as the Maronite, Sunni, Shī'ī, Druze, Greek Orthodox, Protestant, Catholic, and Greek Catholic schools, carry the name of their confession. Others carry the names of the countries or foreign communities supporting them, such as the American Community School, British School, French Frère and Laïque, Italian School, and German School.

The percentage of students in privately owned schools increases with the level of education, from 56 percent at the primary level to 77 percent at the secondary level. Among secondary schools, the foreign ones continue to be the most advanced in Lebanon, attracting the children of most wealthy and influential families.

About 42 percent of pre-university students and 22 percent at the university level are girls.[41] In most of Lebanon the education of girls is considered by traditional parents less urgent than that of boys, since the social structure still imposes demands on sons to support their parents in their old age and, in addition, to be responsible for unmarried sisters. There is also a latent attitude that the girl's place is ultimately at home, and that her image as a homemaker should not be tarnished by excessive "mixing" and learning beyond the "safe" elementary level. This attitude, however, is fast disappearing, and even girls from the most traditional families are becoming teachers, secretaries, or sales girls and are living away from home.

To sum up, education in Lebanon has so far been largely determined by a laissez-faire philosophy which has allowed every confession to conduct its school system and has permitted foreign missionaries to establish schools with a minimum of interference. A minority of Lebanese students attend the public school system; at the university level it is usually those who cannot afford the fees of the private universities who attend the national Lebanese University. The fact that confessional groups manage their own schools tends to emphasize the separateness of each group, and their attempt to ensure a degree of communal identification. Although radical elites denounce the existing educational system for its divisive character and call for a more secular, national, and uniform system, this opinion is not shared by the leading political actors, who genuinely believe that the continuity of the existing liberal order depends on the diversity of outlook associated with confessional education.

Economy

Lebanon's economic system, like its educational system, has been largely conditioned by its strategic location, ethnic heterogeneity, and external contacts. Its generally laissez-faire economy stands in contrast to the growing socialization of the economies of other countries in the Arab world. Its free market, the diversity of its product, and its various invisible incomes (private capital inflows, transportation, and tourism) have been a source of strength and stability to the economy, providing Lebanon with a higher standard of living than most countries in the Middle Eastern region, and continued economic progress in spite of recurrent political crises.

Lebanon's gross national product (G.N.P.) for 1968, the most recent year for which final figures are available, was about L.L. 4,274 million as compared to L.L. 3,309 million for 1964. Estimates of G.N.P. for 1965 and 1966 are put by the Ministry of Finance at L.L. 3,640 and 3,995 million, respectively. Using the 1968 G.N.P. as a standard guide for comparative purposes and allowing for a population estimated by the Ministry of General Planning at close to three million, the G.N.P. per capita is not far from L.L. 1,400 (roughly $500) per year. While this is far behind Europe and North America, it is well above the average for most less-developed regions of the world, where per capita income is often $100 or less.[42] Among Arab countries, only Kuwait and Libya have higher per capita incomes; this, of course, is due to the oil boom of the past two decades.[43] Lebanon's per capita income, higher than all African countries except Libya, French Somaliland, and South Africa, is higher than those of all Asian countries with the exception of Kuwait, Israel, Hong Kong, Singapore, and Japan.

The contribution of the various sectors to the domestic product shows that Lebanon is essentially a service economy.[44] Almost 70 percent of its gross domestic product comes from so-called tertiary sources and only about 25 percent from agriculture and industry. Income from tourism is incorporated with services: commerce, trade, hotels, restaurants, travel agencies, etc. Income from every service category, with the exception of trade, is below 10 percent. This pattern is partly in line with official policy to diversify services and thereby reduce the economy's vulnerability to adverse external fluctuations.[45] Lebanon's dependence on the foreign market is not unlike that of the Arab states—Iraq, Kuwait, Saudi Arabia, and Libya—whose main source of income is from oil exports to Europe.

As in most less-developed countries, the relation between the industry distributions of labor force and G.N.P. by origin is one of great unevenness (see Table 2.2). While half the labor force is in agriculture, its contribution to the national product is a bare 12 percent. In industry the percent of the labor force (11 percent) is little different from its contribution (13 percent) to the national product. In contrast, labor force in commerce and trade, with about the same percent as in industry alone, contributes more to the national product than agriculture and industry combined. These features are not unique to the Lebanese economy, although the extent of these divergences may be higher than in most other countries in the Middle East.

Existence of a free-market economy has led to a large influx of capital from the oil-producing countries in the Middle East and to an economic boom, particularly in Beirut and its suburbs, since the early 1950s. Not all of the influx has been sanctioned

TABLE 2.2

Distribution by Industry Sector of Labor Force and G.N.P., (1966–69 Average Percentages)

Sector	Percent Distribution Labor Force	G.N.P.
Agriculture	50	12
Banking and Insurance	0.4	4
Commerce and Trade	11	33
Government	23	8
Industry	11	13
Others	4.6	30
Total	100	100

Source: Ministry of General Planning.
Note: See also Note 44.

officially; Syrian capital has been smuggled into Lebanon by merchants seeking an escape from stringent legislation. Strict Lebanese legislation concerning banking secrecy, *inter alia*, has also made Beirut a major banking center in the Middle East. Some of the "new capitalists" in the region, especially Saudi and Kuwaiti investors, prefer to deal with Lebanese Arabs, whose language and culture they understand, rather than with European bankers—although shrewdness often dictates that they deal with both.

Lebanon's role as a middleman in international trade was first firmly established during World War II. Lebanese entrepreneurs found new opportunities to supply the needs of the large Allied military force in Lebanon and—unlike the situation during World War I—were sufficient in numbers, skill, and experience to meet the demands of the Allied armies. Thereafter, when oil money from the Peninsula began to flow into Lebanon, Lebanese businessmen were ready with their banking facilities and world-wide contacts to advise the Arab kings and princes about the management of their new wealth. Muslim Lebanese served as advisors and confidants to these princes in their native lands. By virtue of its temperate climate and advanced educational and medical centers, Lebanon has provided the wealthy Saudis, Kuwaitis, Qataris, and Bahrainis with the recreational and personal-care facilities they needed. Oil-rich princes and merchants, encouraged by Lebanese legislation, have bought land in the hills close to Beirut and have built sumptuous residences for summer and weekend visits. To many of them Lebanon has become a second home, a place to open a bank account and establish a business, as well as a haven, or an ultimate insurance policy in the event that radical regimes at home were to topple the traditional ruling class.

Lebanon's weak central government, a government not inclined to impose radical measures of any sort, has provided an added attraction for investment. In the past and today the government has posed no nationalization threat, no potential scare of control to repel the new and insecurely rich barons of the Arab East.

Lebanon's balance of payments on current account is made up of two highly diverse components: on the one hand, because of limited agricultural and industrial output and also because of extensive consumer imports needed for a rapidly developing middle class, Lebanon has a pronounced deficit of trade in goods. On the other hand, there is a surplus in such invisible items as private-capital inflows, transportation services, and tourism.

About 60 percent of Lebanon's imports are from the United States and western Europe, and about 60 percent of its exports are to Arab countries and eastern Europe.

Money sent into Lebanon by individuals, institutions, and governments helps to offset Lebanon's international trade deficit. Receipts from this category have averaged a little over L.L.100 million ($33 million) per year for 1965–70. The nature of these inflows has been changing. In the early 1950s most remittances came from Lebanese emigrants in Africa and the Americas. The emigrants are mostly Christian and their remittances benefited primarily the Christian villages. Since the late 1950s, however, remittances from Lebanese workers and officials working in Middle Eastern oil-producing countries have become as significant as those sent from Africa and the Americas. While there are no figures on the confessions of Lebanese workers in the Middle East countries, the proportion of Muslims among them is known to be very high. Early emigration gave the Christians economic advantages over most of their Muslim brethren. This advantage is being narrowed by short-term emigration of Sunnis to Saudi Arabia and Kuwait and long-term emigration of Shī'īs and Druze to Australia and Canada.

The geographic distribution of the Christians in Mount Lebanon and in Beirut has also been a factor in their economic prosperity because of the attraction for tourists which this area presents. Druze have also benefited from their location, though to a lesser degree. The Sunnis, except in Beirut and, in part, in Sidon or Tripoli, have benefited much less and the Shī'īs in the south have benefited the least.

The business skills of the Lebanese in central Lebanon (Beirut and its mountain environs) and their outside contacts had encouraged tourism even before the government began to invest in the tourist industry. Fifty percent of Lebanon's tourists came from the Arab world, 35 percent from Europe, and 15 percent from the United States.

The service and transit sectors of the economy again benefit mostly central Lebanon. The absence of large-scale industry minimizes work opportunities and discourages mobility. Industry is constrained by the paucity of natural resources.

Industry

While Christians are benefiting most from industrialization in central Lebanon, no one sect has a monopoly on industrial ownership and management. Lebanese industry traditionally has been concentrated in crafts and food processing based upon individually owned and operated productive units. To a large extent it remains so at present. Industrial enterprises, especially those employing few workers, tend to be craft industries operated by an individual or a single family unit. Partly as a result, the traditional guild system, which provided stability and identity to large segments of Middle Eastern society during the past five centuries, has rapidly declined, resulting in a vacuum yet to be filled by the trade-union movement.[46]

The industrial sector has been growing gradually since the Second World War. Between 1958 and 1967 industrial plants have doubled in number, tripled in labor size, and almost quintupled in capital (current prices).

Lebanon has about 6,000 craft and industrial establishments[47] employing approximately 11 percent of the working force. Table 2.3 shows the distribution by size of firm. The majority of these establishments, especially those employing less than five workers, are individual- or family-operated units.

TABLE 2.3
Distribution of Craft Establishments
into Five or More Workers (1969)

No. of Workers	Percent of Establishment
5 to 9	51.4
10 to 24	33.0
25 to 49	8.6
50 and more	7.0
Total	100.0

Note: Data unavailable for under-five establishments.
Source: Ministry of General Planning.

Lebanese industry is concentrated largely in the production of food products, beverages, textiles, furniture, paper, printing materials, chemicals, and electrical products. There are a few large-scale industries, such as the two refineries mentioned earlier, cement factories, and electrical power plants. Table 2.4 shows quantities of production by sector and the pattern of recent growth. Available export data suggest a rapid expansion in the food-processing and textile industries since 1967. The indicated absolute decline in cement production in 1967, reflecting a recession in construction activity, has been reversed more recently.

TABLE 2.4
Value and Index Numbers of Industrial Production (1965–67)

		Values			Index Numbers	
Product	Unit	1965	1966	1967	1966	1967
Cement	1,000 tons	970	1,095	1,016	113	105
Electricity	Million kwh.	582	666	706	114	121
Gasoline	1,000 tons	280	310	303	110	108
Jewelry (gold)	Kg.	2,020	3,150	2,561	156	127
Tobacco Products	Tons	2,432	2,560	2,695	105	111

Source: Ministry of General Planning, *Bulletin Statistique Mensuel.*

Banks have played a relatively minor role in Lebanon's industrial development. In 1965 banks supplied only about 35 percent of total industrial capital outlays made in that year. Although relatively stable politically, Lebanon has not succeeded in attracting significant Western capital for industrial investment. Of the comparatively small amount of non-Lebanese capital invested in industry, 55 percent is Arab (Saudi, Kuwaiti, Syrian), 25 percent European, 9 percent American, and 11 percent comes from diverse foreign groupings.[48]

Capital is generally secured from immediate family savings, the pooled resources of cousins or friends, emigrants, business profits, and foreign speculators. While banks which supply capital at high rates of interest are often available, there is no one major source to supply long-term loans at low interest rates.

Agriculture

Agriculture is the poorest paying sector in the country. It is possible for extensive landowners to depend on agriculture exclusively and be relatively well off, but small landowners who have no income other than that of their land tend to be poor. Populations in the north and South regions of Lebanon are largely rural and Muslim, but in some cases the Christian villages in these two regions are better off economically than the Muslim villages because of investments made by emigrants, or because superior private schools often favor former villages by developing work capabilities permitting their students to be more mobile. Many may go to the city to seek skilled work as clerks or to acquire higher education preparing them for better paying jobs.

Economic disparities are potential sources of tension between the Christian and Muslim communities. The 1958 conflict was in part a conflict between the "haves" and "have nots." President Shihāb's policy to promote planning and development projects in the less prosperous (dominantly Muslim) regions was an attempt to introduce economic readjustment between the generally well-to-do Christian communities and the generally less-well-off Muslim areas.

With 50 percent of its labor in agriculture Lebanon falls into a relatively traditional category when compared on a worldwide basis. It is, however, much less traditional than the rest of the Arab East, where we find 65 percent of the labor force so engaged in Egypt, 75 percent in Iraq, and 70 percent in Syria.[49]

Land ownership varies in size according to geographical location. In the mountainous regions the landholdings are small, while in the plains properties are larger. Large estates employing sharecroppers, common in Egypt, Syria, and Iraq in the 1940s and 1950s, have not been a significant factor in Lebanon for over a century. The pattern of land distribution in the 1950s is detailed in Table 2.5: more than one-fourth of all landowners hold plots less than one-tenth of a hectare, accounting for less than one percent of the agricultural area and conversely 5 percent own plots of four hectares or more, accounting for nearly three-fifths of the area. About 80 percent of the agricultural land is owner-operated, 18 percent being operated by tenants and the rest operated collectively by a village, an institution, or a *waqf* (trust).[50] Lebanon's laissez-faire economy sets few limits on land ownership and no restrictions on the kinds of crops grown.[51] Citizens of Arab countries may purchase land in Lebanon with a minimum of restrictions, though non-Arabs must secure presidential permission.

TABLE 2.5
Distribution of Landowners and Cultivated Area by Size (1950s)

Size (Hectares)	Percent Distribution Owners	Cultivated Area
Under 1/10	27.1	0.9
1/10 to 1/2	37.0	7.8
1/2 to 1	15.2	9.1
1 to 2	9.8	11.9
2 to 4	5.9	13.6
4 to 10	3.4	17.3
10 to 20	0.9	10.4
20 to 40	0.4	11.3
40 and above	0.3	17.7
Total	100.0	100.0

Source: J. Gauthier and E. Baz, "Aspect Général de L'Agriculture Libanaise," République Libanaise, Ministère de l'Agriculture, Tome I (Beyrouth: 1960).

Agricultural progress has been equated with the expanding capacity of farm people to accelerate the national output by supplying their total economy with foods and fibers appreciably faster than population growth adds new mouths to feed.[52] By this measure Lebanese agriculture is rather progressive in fruit production and relatively stagnant in cereal production and livestock farming. Production of agricultural commodities is hindered because of limited markets. The internal market is confined mainly to the middle and lower-middle classes in the urban areas, while rich Lebanese and members of the foreign community consume only a small amount of the local produce, choosing to depend on imported commodities. The very poor farmers produce enough on their land to be relatively free from the market economy.

Lebanon's wheat and barley are no longer adequate for its needs; wheat and other cereals are imported from Syria, Canada, Australia, and the United States. Total agricultural-related imports, including cereals, fruits, vegetables, and agricultural machines, are generally three times as large as agricultural exports. Lebanese exports are hampered by rising costs of agriculture (in particular the need for terracing), scarce available land, and the uneconomical nature of many private family-type operations. The total gross value of agricultural crops in Lebanon has been increasing at an annual rate of about 3.5 percent since 1965; all as a result of rising productivity per acre. Private enterprise in livestock, particularly in the poultry industry, has been developing more rapidly; the production of eggs increased eight-fold between 1958 and 1966. Much of the capital invested in the poultry industry has been accumulated by Lebanese working in the oil-producing countries of the Middle East.

Summary

In both agriculture and industry, developments since independence show that the role of the private sector is growing. The mosaic nature of the educational system has prepared Lebanese of all confessions for diversified economic activities.

Highest economic returns, however, have tended to accrue to the Christians of central Lebanon, thus creating an imbalance that at times has contributed to serious civil conflict (in 1958, for example). The laissez-faire system operating in a multi-confessional society has created conditions that have led to the modernization of central Lebanon and to other pockets in the rest of Lebanon. Growing consciousness of the chasm between central Lebanon and the rest of Lebanon and between the Christians on the one hand and the Muslims on the other has led intellectuals and statesmen alike to ask for government interference to bridge the chasm. The expectation of liberals and intellectuals that government can ensure modernization and equitable distribution of benefits is limited by the laissez-faire tradition of Lebanon's government. The multiplicity of sects, of foci of economic and political power, and of long-held autonomies in the confessions have led to the establishment of a political formula which ensures consensus that moves slowly and that limits the arena of central political action. Nevertheless, government representing all factions can, more than any other organization, relate to all sects, to all educational activities, to all economic enterprises, and therefore legitimately affect change in these areas.

III
Lebanon's Political Formula: Governing by Consensus

The more nearly a country approaches the middle of the spectrum between tradition and modernity the more difficult it is to describe in unequivocal terms. Lebanese politics, like the society it represents, is a mix of tradition and modernity, feudal vestiges[1] and capitalism, confessionalism and secularism, democracy and plutocracy, rugged individualism and narrow communalism. Though every polity is a mix in a sense, having its own unique characteristics, the Lebanese polity is rendered comparatively complex by its religious heterogeneity and labyrinthine history. The roots of the coalition formula stretch back into history, particularly to the mutaṣarrifiyyah regime, and not until the French Mandate and early independence period did it come to acquire more or less its present form.[2]

This chapter attempts to make two points: first, that Lebanon's coalition formula has provided wide political support for political legitimacy, reconciling traditional loci of power with institutional democratic principles; and second, that in the Lebanese context the coalition formula has been conceived of more as an instrument of stability and liberty than of achievement and efficiency. The growing demands put on the formula by intellectuals who have been dissatisfied with the pace of modernization and have sought to transform its polycentric nature to undertake, more efficiently, greater socio-economic functions, represents a major input in contemporary Lebanon. It is too early to determine whether the polity's response to this demand, by instituting development planning and reforming the bureaucracy, will prove adequate. There is no doubt, however, that the political formula has allowed some modernization and incremental change to occur, and has furthered, in varying degrees, aspects of democracy and development. What the political formula is, how it operates, and what role it can play in modernization are some of the questions that this chapter attempts to interpret.

The Mandate introduced a new political structure that was defined in the Constitution of 1926. The Constitution itself, still operative, although several times amended, was written by Lebanese jurists and modelled largely after the French Third Republic in definition of parliamentary, presidential, and cabinet powers. In addition, on the eve of independence a National Pact had been drawn up to clarify further the allocation of powers and offices in the pluralistic-type republic about to be launched.

The Pact defined the shares of the various confessional communities in the formal governmental structure[3] and consisted of a number of basic principles regarding rule of the country and orientation of policy. Essentially an agreement between the Maronite leader, Bishārah al-Khūri, and the Sunni leader, Riyāḍ al-Ṣulḥ, the pact was to promote independence and rally the support of Lebanese communities by providing for a communal sharing of power. It preserved the preeminent position of the Maronites under the French Mandate by allocating to them the presidency; it gave the premiership, the second most powerful post, to the Sunnis; and it allotted the speakership of the parliament to the third largest sect, the Shī'īs. The vice-premiership and the vice-speakership were allotted to the Greek Orthodox. The three presidencies—of the Republic (Christian), of the cabinet, and of the parliament (Muslim)—constitute the triumvirate that reconciles the major groupings.

In these ways a sort of confessional balance has also been maintained in the formulation of policy. Thus, having been assured of the presidency, the Maronites could afford to secure independence from France—the country that had been in close relation with them since the time of the Crusades. Similarly, having secured independence from France, and the premiership the Sunnis could afford to enter into a position of power in the government.

Every major sect is represented in parliament, and small sects like the Jews and Protestants have a representative of minorities. Cabinet size varies with almost every shift in composition. Ministers may head one, two, or more ministries. A large cabinet of 15 or more members may include a member of the Armenian community and it is relatively easy to recruit from all the communities to fill positions in the bureaucracy. However, minorities may be too small to gain representation in the cabinet.

The Pact sought to define external independence by stipulating that the Christian Lebanese should no longer look to the West for protection[4] or the Lebanese Muslims to Syria or to any larger Arab entity.

Success of the formula in preserving independence while maintaining democratic institutions has been no mean feat. This has special import when one considers that the formula was applied in a period in which military regimes were a common alternative to constitutional and parliamentary government. Through the spirit of conciliation that pervades the formula, major conflicts were avoided and stability was maintained. It is partially this stability and the liberal pluralistic order associated with it which has permitted modernization to proceed unhampered.

The application of the formula in the context of the Constitution represents a blending of the secular democratic institutions introduced under the Mandate with native traditional institutions. The Lebanese political process, therefore, is the product of a mix between two differing institutions, or rather two divergent orientations, which has worked and proved capable of progressive adaptation. While democratic institutions have had to accommodate Lebanese values and rules of the game, their very presence has in turn affected the latter. The game is now played within a democratic framework, complete with periodic elections, written constitution, and peaceful successions of governments. The weaknesses that many of the radical elite detect in the game plan are, to an extent, often guarantees against revolutionary short-cuts which could introduce dangers into the fabric of the delicately balanced Lebanese society.

While in many neighboring countries parliament has been rejected as being incapable of meeting rising social demands, Lebanon's coalition formula has preserved the parliament as a legitimate channel for entering political life. In Lebanon the parliament has become a stable institution in which each confessional segment of the heterogeneous Lebanese society is represented. It provides a meeting ground for regional leaders and a platform for national policies. The formula provides for parliamentary representation based on a ratio of six Christians to five non-Christians (Muslims and Druze), with the number always a multiple of eleven. Numbers have varied from 44 to 99 at present. Women have the right to vote and be elected;

however, with the exception of one interim term, no woman has been elected to parliament. Elections take place every four years, by secret ballot and in electoral districts defined by law.

The electoral law has been revised several times and is currently under review by parliament. What is at stake in the reconsideration of the existing law is not only the number of deputies in parliament, but the size of the electoral district, the nature of the electoral list, the deposit required of the candidate, and the very mechanics of the election process.

The parliament is relatively weak. The president, who in agreement with his premier can dissolve parliament, possesses a formidable control over its authority, the usual result of which is compliance of the legislature with his wishes.

The electoral process has been criticized by the radical elite for favoring the rich and the traditional leaders. To become a candidate for parliament, for example, one must deposit with the government L.L.3000 ($1,000), which is forfeited if the candidate receives less than 20 percent of the vote. While intending to limit the number of candidacies, the law in fact represents an obstacle to the peasant and working classes, none of whom has yet been elected to parliament. Another obstacle is the need for an "open house" during election. Hundreds of people must be fed, entertained, talked to, and helped. The candidate must offer loans to the needy, pay newspapers to write favorably about him or to stop them from writing unfavorably. He must pay influential men, *qabadays* (strong men), and other intermediaries who influence small groups, guarantee that they vote the right way, bring out the "right" voters, and block the "wrong" voters on election day. He must have ready cash to buy votes, usually just a few hours before the ballot boxes close, although it is illegal. The za'īms (strong political leaders often with feudal background), have been known to exact hundreds of thousands of Lebanese pounds from wealthy professionals, businessmen, and enterprising ex-bureaucrats who are eager to enter parliament[5]. Such entry is almost assured to the rich if a strong za'īm agrees to include him on his electoral list[6]. In the past, competition for parliamentary seats was limited to the major families with special political influence in their respective areas of origin. One-fourth of the deputies in the 1960 parliament "inherited their parliamentary seats from a scion of their families—a father, an uncle, a grandfather. Of the four deputies in the 1960 parliament who died in office, three were succeeded by their children."[7]

Despite the entrenchment of such traditional norms in parliamentary politics, the electoral scene is slowly changing. Hudson, using indices of voter participation, parliamentary recruitment, and competitiveness in parliamentary electoral contests, concluded that the Lebanese system, in spite of its confessional-traditional base, was moderately capable of modernization.[8] First, voter participation was found to be increasing (voting for parliament in 1964 was 14 percent higher than in 1960). Second, he found a broadening of political recruitment and an increase in the number of presumably more qualified professional people, as shown in Table 3.1.

Based on 276 contests in the six parliamentary elections between 1947 and 1967, Hudson's index of competitiveness in elections shows an upward trend. The winners, unlike the case in highly traditional or dictatorial regimes, came out ahead by clear, but not overwhelming, majorities, an indication of political freedom and of the availability of challengers to entrenched traditional leaders. While the formula favors the well placed, it does not seem to block parliamentary access for new men. With respect to the presidency, although the formula excludes all non-Maronites, the fact that the election is carried out directly

TABLE 3.1

Occupational Distribution of Deputies in Seven Lebanese
Parliaments for Selected Years, 1943–1964*

Occupation	1943	1947	1951	1953	1957	1960	1964
Landlords	46.5	48.2	42.5	40.9	33.3	23.0	23.2
Lawyers	33.9	27.3	25.0	34.1	36.3	29.0	27.3
Businessmen	10.2	10.9	12.5	6.8	1 1.1	14.0	17.2
Professionals	10.2	12.7	20.0	18.2	19.0	34.0	32.3
Totals	100.0	100.0	100.0	100.0	99.7**	100.0	100.0

*Michael Hudson, "The Electoral Process and Political Development in Lebanon," p. 178.
**Discrepancy due to rounding.

by parliament for a six-year term usually ensures the election of experienced men.[9] Of the five presidents elected since independence, the first two were outstanding lawyers, the third was the head of the army (elected to restore normalcy in the wake of the 1958 civil conflict), the fourth was a prominent journalist and diplomat, and the fifth (the incumbent) is a prominent za-'īm and an experienced politician.

Self-interest groups, or clubs, play an important role in electing the president. Typically, the presidential nominee selected is submitted to parliament merely for formal election and legitimization. "Today Parliament will meet to elect Khūri (or Shihāb, etc.)" is a typical election day headline.[10]

The Constitution gives the president substantial powers and a major role in national consolidation assigned to him by tradition. In a society as heterogeneous, polyarchic, and multipoled as Lebanon, the president serves as a catalyst, standing above petty conflicts. He attends both Christian and Muslim religious ceremonies; is expected to speak of "Arabism" to broaden the political outlook of the Christians, and of "Lebanism" to strengthen the concept of a sovereign state among the Muslims;[11] and to extol the brotherhood of all communities, a spirit of tolerance, and the need to strengthen democracy and modernization. While many among the radical elite and the intellectuals oppose limiting the office of president to a particular sect, most prominent leaders of all sects have accepted the existing practice, hesitating to risk changing a formula that has worked for more than three decades.

The president is expected to provide national leadership and to reconcile divergent factions. He performs this delicate function through the cabinet, the mechanism through which prominent representatives of the main confessions are brought together to govern in a spirit of consensus. Since the president selects a prominent Sunni leader to form a cabinet, and since he usually presides over the council of ministers, it is primarily his leadership and only secondarily that of the premier that determines general policy orientation. The formula leaves the ministers at the mercy of the president and premier, who, if they agree, can dissolve the cabinet.

Joining the cabinet has been considered by members of parliament as a way to increase their influence and prestige. Since cabinet membership requires the support of the president, aspirants usually hesitate to oppose him by opposing his selections for cabinet posts, at least on an individual basis. Instead, blocs of a temporary nature may be formed, consisting of clusters of deputies led by a prominent political figure. Each bloc decides whom to support for each cabinet post. For example, at one time a bloc may support candidate X, with the understanding that in the succeeding cabinet, X and his colleagues will support candidate Y, and so on. The advantages of a cabinet position include the opportunity to share in the formulation of policy, control one or more ministries, distribute patronage, and increase one's political influence generally. To some, the cabinet post has been a step toward a successful private business or a flourishing law practice.

In the past, cabinets have not averaged more than ten months of tenure. Nevertheless, elements of stability are afforded by the limited candidature to the premiership[12] and the informal *entente* that usually develops between the president and a Sunni leader.

Concern with consensus and representation of the sects in selection of the cabinet has been accompanied by criticism and obvious weaknesses in operation. At times a person with no notable qualifications is included in the cabinet merely because he satisfies confessional and regional considerations. While no one sect is assigned a particular post in the cabinet (except for the premier and vice premier), a sort of balance is usually maintained between Maronites and Sunnis, Greek Orthodox and Druze, and Greek Catholics and Shī'īs. Sectarian representation in the cabinet, unlike that in the parliament, is not defined by law, but is regulated by custom. Distribution of posts to individual ministers is affected by the size of their sect and the personality of the individual. A purview of Lebanese cabinets formed between 1958 and 1972 shows that they included members with Ph.D. degrees, as well as members with only a secondary education and no specialization; members in their late sixties, as well as those in their thirties; radical and progressive members, as well as conservative and traditional ones. A cabinet can be as qualified as the president and parliament want it to be. Since there is no Constitutional provision that cabinet members should be recruited from parliament (though they usually have been), the president may persuade parliament to approve a cabinet whose members are recruited wholly or partially from outside parliament. However, presidents have made limited use of their option to recruit ministers from universities and the private sector. On the whole, parliament disapproves of this practice and believes that the top political posts should be reserved for its members, for only they are elected by the people and therefore politically accountable. In addition, approximately half the members of parliament hold university degrees (generally in law and medicine); they claim therefore, to be fully qualified to hold these political offices.

It is only when the president finds wide political divergencies among the parliamentary blocs that he resorts to forming a nonparliamentary cabinet. The incumbent president, Suleiman Franjiyyah, selected a prominent Beiruti za'īm and member of parliament, Ṣā'ib Salām, to be premier. After several unsuccessful attempts to form a parliamentary cabinet, President Franjiyyah encouraged Salām to form a cabinet of young, educated, non-political men.[13] This was accomplished and the press immediately dubbed it *ḥukūmat al majhūlīn* (the cabinet of unknowns), and the cabinet of technocrats. The political power of the members of such a cabinet derives almost entirely from the support they receive from the president and his premier. Consequently, it is much easier for the president and premier to manage such a non-parliamentary and non-political cabinet than one made up of za'īms politically strong in their own right. Conversely, a non-political cabinet is more difficult to defend and maintain in the face of parliamentary criticism and attack.

All cabinets since 1958 have emphasized their commitment to development projects. They have emphasized that Lebanon, particularly after the civil conflict of 1958, has needed state intervention to improve economic conditions outside central Lebanon and to bridge the economic gap between Christians and Muslims. Development has been accepted by intellectuals as an essential part of the governing formula. The Constitution and Pact have been described as empty shells if they fail to provide social and economic benefits which they believe are largely the criterion for imparting legitimacy upon governments.[14]

Adequate examination of the governing formula must also take into consideration its day-to-day operation through clubs, a term chosen to indicate amorphous groupings and classifications of interests rather than organizations with formal structure and hierarchy. The clubs are cliques or groups that share common interests and apply pressure on the systems to ensure the continuation of such interests. Often the common denominator shared by the members of a certain club is too subtle to be readily observed by outsiders. The various clubs can be classified under the headings of za'īm, military, ecclesiastic, embassy, business, and intellectual. Since the clubs are largely unorganized and the literature on the subject is nonexistent, they are treated here largely on the basis of observation and direct knowledge.

Za'īm Club

Perhaps the most important club consists of the za'īms.[15] These leaders control major blocs in parliament and exercise such great powers in their respective regions that they can maintain some autonomy in the face of the central government, as was demonstrated in 1958. During that conflict, while central authority practically collapsed, entire quarters in Beirut were under the effective rule of Ṣā'ib Salām; Tripoli was controlled by Rashīd Karāmi and the Shūf area by Kamāl Junblāṭ. All of these leaders were za'īms. The poorer the people in a community and the stronger their confessional loyalty, the stronger is the position of the za'īm. While the za'īm is essentially a political figure who must protect his followers, find jobs for them, and help them financially when they are in need, he is not without religious charisma. A zaʿīm of a Druze area must, by necessity, be a Druze; of a Sunni area, a Sunni, and so on. This is because political loyalty follows confessional lines. The zaʿīm can always count on his followers to respond to his wishes irrespective of whether these are reasonable or unreasonable. His followers owe allegience to him by virtue of his person, family, and place in society and not necessarily because of his personal achievements. Indeed, personal achievement in the form of intellectual excellence or professional standing might work against him if it introduced norms of behavior that conflict with the people's expectations of their zaʿīm. Accordingly, the Druze leader, Kamāl Junblāṭ, who is a man of high intellectual achievement, is forced, in his role as zaʿīm, to behave toward his community as a feudal leader, thus violating certain rational principles in which he believes. If he does not act in his community as expected, he is likely to lose the reverence in which he is held by the Druze community. Zaʿīms tend to be wealthy, being heirs of prominent families that have had, often since Ottoman times, if not before, extensive political and economic influences in the country. Indeed, the concept of zaʿīm is closely associated with the notion of a feudal system, one in which tenants depend completely on their landlord, consider him their leader who becomes, in effect, the pivot of their lives—socially, politically, and economically.

That Lebanon, one of the most modernized countries in the Arab world, has accommodated the zaʿīm institution to a parliamentary system, is a remarkable instance of historical continuity and change.

While sometimes disagreeing on issues, zaʿīms cooperate to the extent necessary to perpetuate their power as the ruling class, indeed as the main political actors since independence in Lebanon. They determine the election of presidents, the formation of cabinets, and the adoption of policies. As a group, this club's commitment to modernization varies with the assessment of its members as to how modernization would affect their power position. Commitments therefore tend to be opportunistic rather than consistent or based on ideology. While a few za'īms have opposed the spread of education in their regions fearing its impact on political objectives and traditions, development projects that would increase za'īm wealth, prestige, and political power have been supported.

Military Club

Although Lebanon, since independence, has been able to maintain the supremacy of the civil order, armies have always played decisive political roles in the Middle East.[16] The current role of the military club in Lebanon reflects the fact that in the past decade, largely as a result of political developments in Syria, Jordan, Iraq, Israel, and Egypt, army officers in Lebanon have begun to participate discreetly in politics. Their influence increased greatly when General Shihāb assumed the presidency. During the previous decade, the army both interfered in the electoral process, and through its intelligence arm, the Deuxième Bureau, affected recruitment into the bureaucracy and promotion within it. Since the army is only one force among many, it has tended to exercise its power through persuasion or in "association" with leading members of the za'īm class. Nevertheless, there has been substantial ideological commitment among its leaders to modernization ideals largely as a result of their training and social standing.[17] According to studies undertaken in France, Britain, and the United States, most Lebanese army officers are highly trained specialists in technical matters.

The role of the military club in Lebanese politics in the 1970s is now very much in question. Its 1970 candidate for the presidency, Eliyās Sarkīs, was supported by 49 out of the 99 members of parliament and lost, and it is now clear that the *entente* between the military and the supporters of Shihāb in parliament (known as al-Nahj) is rapidly dissolving. The Franjiyyah regime (1970–76) has severely restricted the activity of the Deuxième Bureau (the intelligence office of the army) and dispersed its leading officers who had wielded great power under Shihāb and Ḥilu, by sending them abroad to serve as military attachés in European, African, and Latin American countries. Various measures purporting to restrict the power of the army in internal affairs have been undertaken. President Franjiyyah, supported by the Tripartite Alliance—a loose political grouping made up of the three right-wing parties—the Katā'ib (Phalange) of Pierre Jumayyil, the National Bloc of Raymond Eddeh, and the Liberal Party of Kamīl Sham'ūn is committed to the policy of strengthening civil control over the military; consequently, the powers of the military club are expected to be greatly weakened.

Ecclesiastic Club

Unlike the army officer, who has tended to be a participant in disguise in Lebanese politics, the ecclesiastic (bishop, shaykh, priest) has had a long-accepted and respected position in the political history of kaleidoscopic Lebanon. The governing formula recognizes the rights of the heads of the communities to defend the prerogatives of their followers, to make representations to the president and premier on their behalf, and to watch for their proper share in the distribution of offices in the cabinet and in the bureaucracy. Such functions are often executed by means of the ecclesiastic club.

Ecclesiastic heads of the communities are often consulted by the president in the formation of cabinets, and by the cabinet in making appointments to the bureaucracy. Often bishops and shaykhs are asked to submit lists of candidates from their communities to fill a vacancy in the bureaucracy. Za'īms and religious heads often work closely within their respective communities. Maronite leaders cultivate the friendship of the Maronite Patriarch; Sunni leaders cultivate the Mufti of the Republic; Shī'ī leaders cultivate the Shī'ī Imām.

The ecclesiastic club is essentially heterogeneous and polycentric, with each head pulling in the direction of his own community, and each aspiring to political, social, and economic advantages that would accrue benefits to his followers. With long experience, however, there has been a rise of common goals, rituals, and symbolisms consistent with confessional pluralism. Heads of communities exchange visits during each other's religious feasts and meet as conciliators and peacemakers during periods of political tension. The primary commitments of the ecclesiastic club have been to stability, coexistence, peaceful change, preservation of religious values, rather than directly to economic and social development. On the other hand, there is no evidence that the growing modernization of various aspects of the Lebanese polity since independence has weakened the role of the ecclesiastic club, and indeed, some reason to believe that its power is increasing, due to the growing roles of the Mufti (since 1958) and of the Imām (since 1969).[18]

Embassy Club

Embassies of large countries can play a preponderant role in the internal politics of small countries. This is particularly true of Lebanon because of its demography and geography. The strong linkages that the various communities have developed with external powers to which they may relate through religion and culture have provided an inevitable basis for foreign influence. Over the years the French, American, British, Egyptian, and Soviet embassies have all developed effective connections with Lebanese political figures.[19] Although no one embassy has been able to play a preponderant role since independence, and indeed it is difficult to define precisely the role of any, a considerable potential for political power exists through explicit or implicit concessions made to them, ironically by the leading Lebanese political actors themselves.

Despite the fact that foreign powers are involved in technical aid to Lebanon and in providing experts on request, on the whole they have not been directly concerned with modernization. Their own interests have usually had a much wider, Middle Eastern context, extending far beyond the frontiers of Lebanon. The role of the embassies in Lebanon accordingly has been highly complicated, dependent on a mixture of national, regional, and international foci, dealing not only with Lebanon but also with its neighboring states and other regions.

Business Club

The separate influence of the business club (the millionaires of Beirut) on the governing process is complicated by the fact that the zaʿīms are wealthy men, and hence associated with the business club by marriage, business, and social life. Nevertheless, the relation of this club with modernization and development is unusually clear and direct. As owners of industrial and commercial firms, large landholdings, and service organizations, the members of this club are closely linked with modernization activities and policies. In all political systems money becomes translated into power. Lebanon's entrepreneurs and traders participate in the governing process in many ways, by running for a seat in parliament, by helping finance those who would favor their liberal economic policy, and by cultivating the attention of presidents, premiers, and cabinet ministers. Through the services of a pertinent bureaucrat, they may evade, delay, or "bend" a policy measure they consider contrasting to their interests. Ideologically, unlike the preceeding clubs, this club believes in laissez-faire, has no interest in planning, and little faith in the ability of the government to intervene in favor of development, although its motivation for profit need not be undermined by modernization. The absence of a strong philanthropic spirit in Lebanon and fear of business risks have encouraged businessmen to invest abroad and have weakened their interest in social welfare. Unless a radical regime (a dubious possibility at present) replaces the existing one, the influence of this club is likely to endure.

Intellectual Club

Finally, reference must be made to the intellectual club, which here refers to all the organized clubs, societies, youth groups, and organizations which intellectuals have established as forums for the voicing of their opinions. A brief sampling of these would include the *Cénacle Libanais,* the Institute of Developmental Studies, the Lebanese Association of University professors, The November 22 Club, the Lawyers Syndicate,

Doctors Syndicate, University Graduates Society, and Lebanese Student League. Highly educated men from among the zaʿīms or members of parliament may be involved also.

Unfortunately for Lebanon's intellectuals, the governing formula leaves little room for them. The political offices which they seek largely are preempted by zaʿīms and their followings. Although their organized clubs provide a liberal forum in which they may speak their mind, the clubs do not assure them of jobs or afford them the opportunity to participate significantly in policy deliberations. Accordingly, the intellectual club has tended to be reserved towards the governing formula and critical of the zaʿīm class and of the slow pace of modernization. Their importance is mainly as critics, though it cannot be denied that their recommendations are considered. Development planning and bureaucratic reforms in the past have been, in part, a response to popular dissatisfaction in which intellectuals were conspicuous. Nevertheless, and curiously enough intellectuals seem to be encouraged and applauded in a way which deprive them of effectiveness, a policy humourously known in Beirut salons as *tanfīs* (literally, drawing the air out). While this assures Lebanon a degree of political freedom and makes it in effect a haven for intellectuals in the Arab East, it provides little real political muscle for internal reform.

Finally, discussion of Lebanon's guiding political formula is not complete without reference to the political parties. These are rightly discussed after the clubs because their influence on the governing process is more limited, although leaders of some of these parties (Kamāl Junblāṭ and Raymond Eddeh, for example) exercise greater power in their capacities as zaʿīms than as heads of parties. Lebanon has a relatively large number of political parties to represent its communities and a wide range of ideological positions. By remaining subservient to confessional loyalties, despite the claims found sometimes in their by-laws, the party as a political institution has failed to influence the political process seriously. Of a total of 99 members in the parliament elected in 1964, only about one-fourth were party members. Although party representation in parliament has been growing, the shift has not been consistent. A rise from 13 percent in 1951 to 24 percent in 1953 was followed by an 18 percent in 1957, and then to a rise again to 35 percent in 1960. Their representation stands now at about 30 percent.

The most important political parties in Lebanon today emerged in the 1930s from boy scout movements or youth organizations formed under the French Mandate. These include the Katā'ib, Najjadah, and the Syrian Social Nationalist Party (SSNP). The Katā'ib, emphasizing the independence of Lebanon and its unique character as an entity separate and distinct from surrounding Arab countries, is essentially a Maronite party with no significant Muslim following. Its Muslim counterpart, the Najjadah, emphasizes the Arab character of Lebanon and is essentially a Sunni party with no significant Christian following. The SSNP stresses the unity of the Fertile Crescent consisting of Lebanon, Palestine, Jordan, Iraq, and Syria. Despite its strongly secular philosophy, it consists largely of Greek Orthodox and other minority groupings.

The only other parties today whose origins date back before independence are a small communist party,[20] three exclusively Armenian parties, and two quasi-parties (the Constitutional Union and the National Bloc) which originally operated as parliamentary blocs but became political parties in the mid-1950s.

A number of new parties appeared after independence. The Muslim Brethren (1949), *'Ibad al-Raḥman* (The Servants of God) (1950), and the Muslim Group (1964) are, as their names indicate, Muslim political organizations with pan-Arab and pan-

Islamic affiliations. The National Appeal (1945), National Organization (1950) and the Arab Nationalist Movement (1950) are predominantly Sunni; they all lack organizational structure. The Arab Resurrection Socialist Party (Ba'th) (1952) is an extension of the original party founded in Syria; its membership is drawn from Sunni, Shī'ī, and a small number of Greek Orthodox and Druze groups. The Progressive Socialist Party (PSP) with a liberal, secular, and socialist ideology is largely a Druze party headed by the prominent Druze leader, Kamāl Junblāṭ. The National Liberals (1959), the party of ex-President Sham'ūn, is predominantly Maronite.

All parties have very limited membership and an undetermined following; none has reliable records. While the Katā'ib and the National Liberals claim large followings, of up to 50,000 each, most other parties claim memberships of about 10,000. Active and dues-paying members are rarely more than a few thousand in any Lebanese party, although each has larger numbers of sympathizers.

The average Lebanese generally shuns party membership and prefers a client relationship with a za'īm. Traditionally the prestige of parties *(aḥzāb)* has not been high, but modernity is slowly changing this attitude and parties have become a factor in public discussions of major issues which can mobilize their followers and can execute strikes.[21]

A brief look at the characteristics all parties tend to have in common, in spite of their diversity, is relevant for an appreciation of their political role. All tend to have strong leaders, who are often their founders. While the principle of periodic election of a leader is maintained, the same person is generally returned to power. To have a Jumayyil, a Junblāṭ, or a Sham'ūn voted out would be tantamount to rebellion.[22] All seem to possess confessional contours and attract mainly adherents from the same religious following as that of the leader. The multiplicity of political parties in Lebanon is in part caused by the multiplicity of communities.

Being small and under the autocratic control of prominent leaders, the parties discourage divergence of views. Political platforms are usually unanimously adopted, as a rule endorsing the leader's policies. Almost all are poorly organized, generally inactive between parliamentary elections, and make little or no effort at continuous propaganda. Only a handful of members in the top echelons meet on a regular basis with the leader and help him in formulating partly policies with respect to issues as they arise.

Almost all have an executive council headed by the leader. The council elects the leader and acts as his advisory board in party management and public policy formulation. Party conferences, such as would allow for grass roots participation, are not usual.

All of Lebanon's parties have tended to be "schizophrenic," i.e., formally modern, but behaviorally traditional. This may be changing soon, however, with transformations which may strengthen the party bureaucracies seemingly bound to occur with the passing of the founding leaders.[23]

Although until now Lebanon's parties often have been modern expressions of traditional power bases, they have in some cases promoted the political careers of intellectuals who would otherwise have had little chance to share in the political process. In reaching beyond the confessional group (and all of them claim to be extra-confessional) to the national public (which barely exists), they may promote the rise of a national public and therefore contribute to national consolidation. Since most of them are modelled on European ideologies—nationalist, liberal democratic, socialist—they tend to graft such ideologies on to the traditional Lebanese base and thereby create a ferment for modernization. For example, the Druze who is a member of the Progressive Party of Kamāl Junblāṭ is directly pitted against a secular socialist ideology that represents, ideologically, an antithesis of his feudal society.

Lebanon's political parties and clubs have both provided access to politically conscious groupings and broadened the arena of political participation, in both cases by providing informal channels for sharing in the governing process. These, along with the electoral system, have so far provided stability, with minor interruptions, and have minimized communal distrust. Both rest largely on the achievement of consensus, through broad representation of views and continuous consultation with political leaders in parliament, religious leaders, business associates, experts, influential outsiders, and intellectuals. Both seek in varying degrees the preservation of the system, strengthening of national unity, and the assurance of basic freedoms for all the groupings.

Because of personalistic and factional aspects of Lebanese politics, considerable political energy must be consumed in jockeying for power, balancing the distribution of power among many players, and achieving tacit agreement on the promotion of tolerance, stability, and the democratic values essential for the continuity of the game.

Although the rules of this game are well known to the players, they make heavy claims on the time of the players and leave inadequate time or room for modernization politics. This is not to say that the existing formula cannot undertake development projects, or act according to objective criteria, or transcend confessional considerations in search of national interest. It can, and it has. But it can do these things only, as it has been doing, within the confines of the formula; cautiously, hesitantly, haphazardly, and inconsistently. Such muddling through may be the only course that Lebanon can follow. Many intellectuals, some of the major political players, and all the radical elite, however, believe that the political formula should be changed to increase the capabilities of government to undertake full-scale modernization.

Chapters IV and V will examine the government's attempt to increase its modernization capabilities by reforming the bureacuracy and introducing development planning. Although the government has not been inactive in other areas, the limits of the formula's capability to institute change are best tested in these two fields.

IV

Bureaucracy in Transition

Reforming the bureaucracy and instituting development projects under the mantle of planning have been two important responses of the Lebanese government to modernizing needs. Governmental response to the need for better housing, education, agriculture, industry, tourism, and welfare services of all kinds must be implemented by the bureaucracy. Hence, for over a decade Lebanon's successive cabinets have been attempting changes in the national bureaucracy that would enable them both to implement the development projects more effectively and to raise the level of public service more generally.

Since the short terms of cabinets resemble a game of musical chairs intended to accommodate as many players as possible for short intervals, the national bureaucracy assumes special importance, in both the formulation and the execution of modernization policies, and, more broadly, as the permanent advisory and policy-making body of the political formula. Bureaucracy as used in this study refers to all government officials, particularly top personnel who are advisors in policy formulation or heads of administrative units in policy implementation.

Studies on Middle Eastern bureaucracies are scarce, and impressions become important in the absence of hard data. Most of the studies which do exist are Ph.D. or M.A. theses or unpublished reports.[1] In Lebanon, as elsewhere, suspicion, legalism, and a pervasive cynical attitude render the collection of data extremely difficult. The analysis in this chapter, therefore, though partly based on official reports, must rely heavily on intensive interviews with bureaucrats and visits to government offices between 1967 and 1972.

It will be seen that the bureaucracy, like the governing bodies, is restricted by personal, factional, and confessional considerations. As a result, it can make only limited contributions to modernization.

Distribution and Relation to Political Formula

The Lebanese bureaucracy has grown with the increasing responsibilities of the state from 4,000 employees in 1930 to about 25,000 at present. In 1930 the affairs of the state were managed by six ministries. At present they are managed by 16, and there is growing pressure to institute more ministries to cope with new demands. The chart on page 78–79 lists the existing ministries and their attached units. As Table 4.1 shows, the ministries vary greatly in size, from 105 officials in Labor and Social Affairs to over 14,000 in National Education. Civil employees in the Ministry of Defense are very few (as a matter of policy the Ministry of Defense does not release data about its composition). The accountability of civil employees is not clearly defined. Article 53 of the Constitution states that the president appoints all officials except those whose method of appointment is otherwise defined by law. Presidential appointments require the signature of the prime minister and the approval of the cabinet. The president is not the head of the bureaucracy, nor is the prime minister. Rather the cabinet, as a council of ministers presided over by the president, controls the bureaucracy, acting as its manager and supervisor.

At times, when it has received special enabling legislation from parliament, the council of ministers can waive the tenure of officials and dismiss the corrupt and inefficient among them. Although bureaucrats once appointed tend to be entrenched, often beyond reach, the council of ministers holds ultimate control over them through its power to fire and transfer. On the

TABLE 4.1

Distribution of Lebanese Civil Service by Ministry, 1965 and 1969*

Agency	1965	1969
Presidency of the Republic	12	12
Office of the Prime Minister	26	36
Civil Service Council	62	75
Central Inspection Administration	180	186
Court of Accounts	48	50
General Disciplinary Council	8	10
Ministry of Justice	118	663
Ministry of Interior	285	468
Ministry of Foreign Affairs and Emigrants	194	226
Ministry of Finance	1,358	1,433
Ministry of Public Works and Transportation	1,165	1,245
Ministry of National Education	10,454	14,060
Ministry of Water and Electrical Resources	91	144
Ministry of National Economy	115	163
Ministry of Post, Telegraph, and Telephone	3,311	3,457
Ministry of Labor and Social Affairs	74	105
Ministry of Tourism	80	119
Ministry of Information	276	313
Ministry of General Planning	113	120
Ministry of Agriculture	427	529
Ministry of Public Health	764	813
Total	19,161	24,227

*Excludes civil employees of Ministry of Defense for which data are unknown.

Source: Data provided by the Civil Service Council.

Presidency of the Republic

Council of Ministers

- Court of Accounts
- Civil Service Council
- Central Inspection Administration
- General Disciplinary Council
- National Council for Scientific Research

- Ministry of Information
  - National Council of Tourism
- Ministry of Tourism
- Ministry of Public Health
- Ministry of National Education and Fine Arts
- Ministry of National Defense
- Ministry of National Economy
- Ministry of Justice
- Ministry of Foreign Affairs and Emigrants

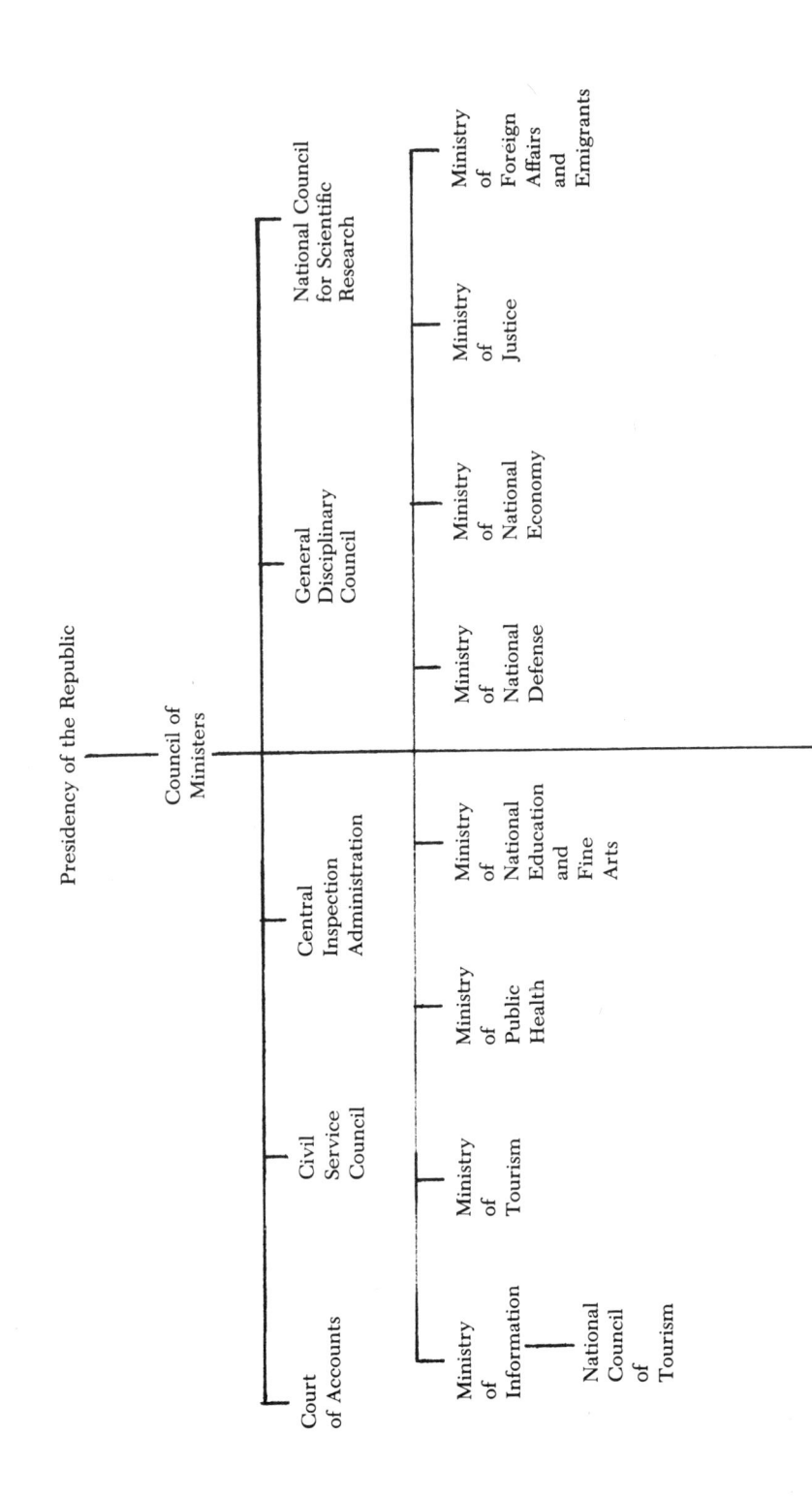

```
├── Ministry of Interior
│   └── Council for the Execution of Major Projects for the City of Beirut
├── Ministry of Finance
├── Ministry of General Planning
├── Ministry of Agriculture
│   ├── Fruit Office
│   ├── Green Plan
│   ├── Silk Office
│   └── Animal Production Office
├── Ministry of Post Telegram and Telephone
├── Ministry of Water and Electrical Resources
├── Ministry of Labor and Social Affairs
│   └── Social Development Office
└── Ministry of Public Work and Transportation
    └── Council for the Execution of Development Projects
```

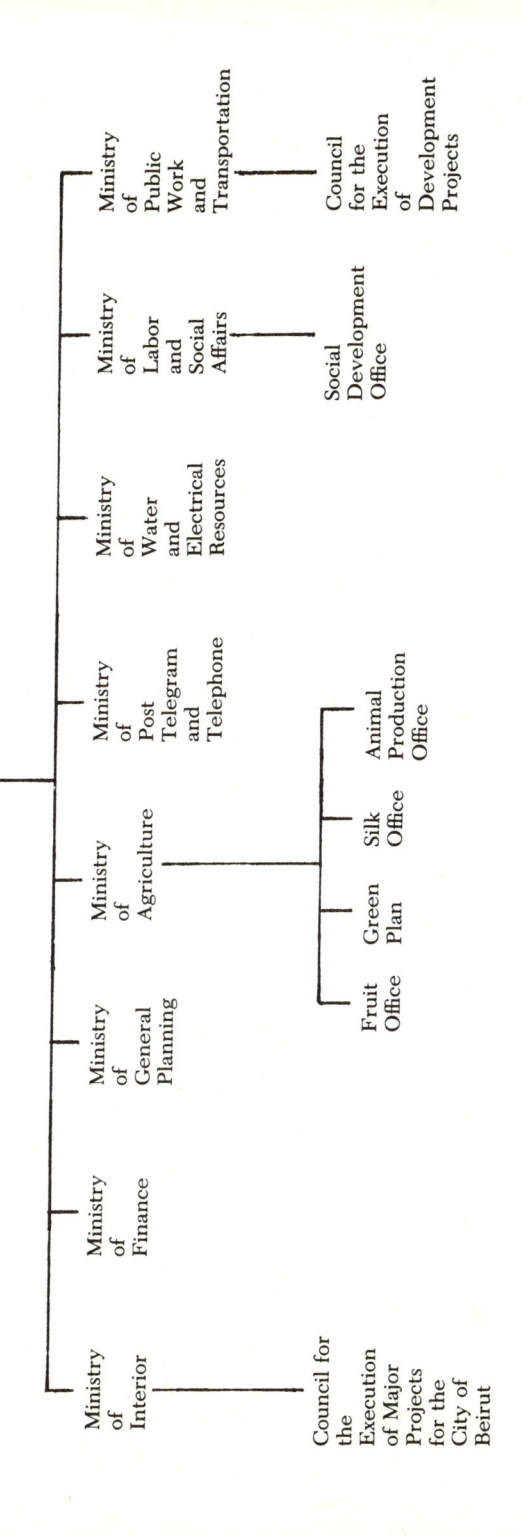

whole the political class which dominates the cabinet and the bureaucratic class have strong social, political, and economic linkages which minimize in practice the legal accountability of the latter.

The politicians who usually head ministries are usually so involved in political manoeuvring that they depend heavily on upper bureaucrats (directors-general of ministries and directors of services) to formulate programs and manage the affairs of their respective ministries. Upper bureaucrats, therefore, play key roles in the execution of policy. They can speed those policy measures they approve or slow down or arrest those which they dislike. This group includes about two hundred people having their origins in all income classes.

Since upper bureaucrats are permanent while cabinets change frequently, and since ministers depend heavily on bureaucrats for policy formulation and execution, an examination of the bureaucracy, especially the upper ranks, is necessary for any study of modernization in Lebanon.

Characteristics of Upper Bureaucracy

The relative stability of the Lebanese system, entrenchment of the wealthy families, and continued reverence for old age and experience give the bureaucratic sections of Lebanese society, like its political and parliamentary sections, a relatively old look. In 1967 I personally interviewed about half of the upper bureaucrats, spending an average of one hour per interview. The interviews were wide ranging, dealing with reasons for joining the bureaucracy, attitudes towards citizens and superiors, roles played in decision-making, etc. I did not ask the interviewees to fill in a questionnaire, a process they might have resented. Hence, I used my interviews as guides, having made extensive notes once the interview was ended.

The great majority of upper bureaucrats are over 50 years of age and well educated, most being graduates of Saint Joseph University. Almost all of them speak French fluently and a few know English in addition to Arabic. French continues to be used in conversation and provides the bureaucratic intelligentsia a channel to Western thought.

The education of these bureaucrats, however, does not free them of the formalism and ritualism prevailing in the traditional Lebanese culture. In their relations with the public, they reflect many of the traditional attributes which hinder the effective operation of modern governmental services.

The upper level bureaucrat considers himself a bey, an effendi, or a za'īm, one entitled to a possession of an office equipped with employees who are there as an entourage to act as subordinates revolving around him and remaining dependent on his good graces.

In interviews the upper bureaucrats tended to agree that the president held the key to the formulation and execution of policy with parliament and the cabinet subservient to him in practice. They ranked themselves second to the president in responsibility for policy formulation and execution. But they blamed politicians, outside influences, or public apathy for policy failures. The attitudes of bureaucrats change in accordance with their rank, training, and social status.

On the basis of personal observation, I have identified five bureaucratic types (below). No particular significance need be associated with this number; types may be grouped together or further subdivided depending on purpose and approach.

Stereotype Categories

1. *The Petty Official.* Belonging to the lowest rungs of the bureaucratic ladder, the petty official usually holds an ele-

mentary school certificate, is a clerk, and is married with a large family. His appearance, judging from his tie, shirt, and suit (all important criteria of status in the Lebanese bureaucracy), usually betray his limited means. His skills are principally clerical and he is accustomed both to accommodating his superiors and to benefiting from the citizenry. Petty officials must cater to their superiors, whose personal favor is needed and whose protection is essential for reaping rewards beyond the strict confines of the law. The efficient, quick performance of a service to an appreciative citizen is expected and likely to earn him a tip or gift. He is likely to remain a petty bureaucrat all of his life, since the paucity of jobs and his limited education leave him few other choices. As a kind of front man he must learn to work with the front men of other bureaucracies, public and private.[2]

2. *The Petty Intellectual.* Consisting of school teachers on the state payroll, and as a rule holders of the Baccalaureate and Brevet certificates, this category draws from the lower middle class. The petty intellectual tends to be a successful member of an extended family who, through his own effort, has received an education and secured government employment. On a salary of about L.L.300 ($100) per month he is expected to support his own family; furnish a house; buy a car, refrigerator, and television; often support his father and mother; and maintain outward signs of material comfort as evidence of his success. Ideological inroads into their ranks by the communist, SSNP, and Arab Nationalist parties have at times encouraged the petty intellectuals to go on strike against the Ministry of National Education, under whose supervision they fall as elementary and secondary-school teachers.

3. *Traditionally Oriented Petty Official.* The traditional bureaucrat, lacking in academic qualifications, usually

owes his position to an influential za'īm,[3] although the practice of flooding the bureaucracy with unqualified employees as a means of solving employment problems is less serious in Lebanon than in other parts of the Arab East.[4] The more closely one relates to the traditional bureaucrat, either directly through family connection or friendship, or indirectly through *wāsṭah* (intercession of an influential friend or za'īm) the more response one tends to get, and vice versa.

The traditional official fits the caricature often depicted of the bureaucrat as clean and tidy, a newspaper in hand, a shoe-shine man at his feet and an errand boy serving him. The acceptance of bribes and presents is conventional, provided these are offered with style, for the image of the bureaucrat as a "clean" person, not susceptible to bribery, must be kept intact. He has a vested interest in making the bureaucratic process mysterious and complex to the average citizen, since this extends his power and the benefits he can derive from it. His reading consists of newspapers. He enjoys politics more than administration, and he thrives in a coffee-house atmosphere in which he can perform services for his political patron. Motivation to improve himself or his office professionally usually is lacking.

4. *High-Level, Modernist Official.* This type includes the university graduate who tends to occupy a top position in the bureaucracy and is anxious to follow a middle course between professional commitment and accommodation to a lax system. As a result he tends to be overworked, being caught between the concentration of powers in his hands and the inefficiency of his subordinates. His salary, about L.L.1,000 a month ($335), is not adequate to finance his social responsibilities, so that he usually must contrive to get himself appointed to numerous governmental committees whose compensation is pro-

rated by the frequency of their sessions; such a practice may at times lead to corruption and administrative overloading.

The modern bureaucrat's typical concern with clothes and emoluments of office may be attributed to a latent anti-intellectualism or a reaction, very often, to his humble origins. Emoluments may take the form of large offices, expensive rugs, impressive desks, a number of telephones, and a gatekeeper to ensure distance from the citizenry.[5]

To maintain a vestige of academic prestige, the modern bureaucrat usually secures part-time employment as a lecturer at one of the universities in Beirut. The faculties of some universities and colleges in Beirut consist largely of bureaucrats who are too involved to have either the time or interest to develop serious curricula or research interests.[6]

The high-level modern official works closely with the political leadership, which is needed to assure promotions, maintain or secure desired positions, and provide entry into the parliament and nominations to the cabinet.

5. *The Radical.* The fifth category, radical, consists of individuals emerging from among the most efficient members of the high-level modern group. The radical often rejects established procedures and bureaucratic patterns. Some are known to have refused to have chairs in their offices in order to eliminate the habit of "sitting and talking," or have conducted administrative business with other bureaucrats while on their feet in order to convey a sense of urgency. Others may refuse to have newspapers, coffee, and "hangers-on" in their offices. Some take the trouble to answer their own telephones, and do so courteously. While the radicals are a small minority, they may—if they can sustain their drive—succeed in causing a new and fruitful ferment in the bureaucracy by serving as pacesetters and models for other bureaucrats. Hope for bureaucratic

reform from the inside rests with these radicals and with the moderns who occupy key posts.

While the radical reformers in the bureaucracy are few in number, their responsibility and potential for effecting change are substantial. Many premiers have said privately that the entire administrative burden in Lebanon lies on the shoulders of a dozen men; they add that if this number could somehow be increased fivefold, Lebanon's bureaucratic structure could become enormously more effective. While this opinion may be argued, there is no doubt that the bureaucracy needs to be rejuvenated continuously and extensively. Lebanese bureaucratic employees on the whole are not sufficiently capable as yet to spearhead modernization policies. Many development projects have often been delayed or poorly executed because of inefficient bureaucratic supervision. A number of major bottlenecks will need to be removed before the bureaucracy can assume a greater role in modernization.

Bottleneck Problems

Two categories of bottlenecks may be usefully distinguished here, one administrative and the other socio-cultural. As a rule, the former are easier to resolve than the latter in that they can be overcome directly through legislation. Socio-cultural bottlenecks, in contrast, may be so deeply rooted in custom and traditional behavior that they defy legislative correction.

1. *Administrative Bottlenecks*

Administrative bottlenecks are the institutional and behavioral patterns that impede the effectiveness of the bureaucracy and consequently hinder its contribution to modernization.

a. *Centralization.* The Lebanese bureaucratic structure, modelled like the French, is highly centralized. Minor administrative matters from outlying areas tend to be referred to the capital, slowing the bureaucratic process, overburdening and depriving the upper-level bureaucrats of opportunities to assume more creative administrative roles. Lower-level bureaucrats rely excessively on their superiors, thereby diminishing even their local effectiveness. Lebanese often complain of administrative circuitousness—the large number of offices they must visit and long list of signatures they must collect before a routine transaction can be completed.[7] Upper bureaucrats are as involved in routine as are the petty bureaucrats and must affix their signatures to hundreds of ordinary transactions daily. Decentralization and deconcentration of powers have been mistrusted because it is believed that local officials tend to be too inexperienced to assume final responsibility for administrative action, a point of view which is both self-justifying and self-defeating.

b. *Outmoded System.* Added to excessive centralization and concentration are bottlenecks in financial administration, employee training, and personnel. Budgeting is inadequately related to program planning. The Ministry of Finance and the Court of Accounts exercise unusually detailed controls over day-to-day expenditures. The hand methods of accounting used are slow. Educational preparation for bureaucratic positions has been limited and is too classical to meet practical needs.[8]

Many laws designed to modernize the bureaucracy have been passed in the last decade but not all have been put into effect. New positions are often left unstaffed, presumably because of budgetary considerations. Role duplication is pervasive. Information available to one ministry does not systematically and routinely flow to others, not only because of inefficiency, but also at times because of the personal and political rivalries of ministers.[9] Poor coordination between offices may place the burden of completing a transaction on the citizen, who may have to follow his transaction personally from office to office.

c. *Technical.* Still other administrative bottlenecks may be physical and technical. Inadequate buildings, rudimentary storage facilities, and antiquated filing systems are standard elements on the Lebanese bureaucratic scene. Lack of central heating or air conditioning, poor lighting facilities, and inadequate office furnishing contribute to low morale.[10] The offices of many directorates are interspersed throughout the city, thereby hindering control and supervision and making for more complicated procedures for the public. Machines such as typewriters, calculators, or computers are not available in sufficient number, partially as a result of budgetary limitations. But, in addition and perhaps more important, the bureaucracy is unable to use effectively the machines it has or to respond to the potentials of modern office technology. Although a computer has been introduced in the Directorate of Central Statistics and typewriters, calculators, and other modern office equipment are found in a number of offices, a great amount of work—even financial computation—is still done by hand, thus perpetuating the traditional handicaps of slowness and inaccuracies.

2. Socio-Cultural Bottlenecks

Socio-cultural bottlenecks are the deeply imbedded customs and attitudes of the people which form traditional barriers against rapid modernization and which determine the orientation of the government and the bureaucracy.

a. *Confessionalism:* Since confessionalism, nepotism,

bribery, and an attitude of laxity all have deep roots in the fabric of Lebanese society, it is not surprising that political administration faces pervasive obstacles to effectiveness.

The Lebanese Constitution is ambivalent regarding the role of confessionalism in the bureaucracy. Article 12 guarantees the right of the Lebanese citizen to hold office on the basis of merit and competence, but Article 95 provides for equitable representation of all the sects in state offices. The latter itself is ambivalent, stating both that such representation is "a temporary measure for the sake of justice and amity" and that it is to continue, "provided it does not endanger the public interest." As a result, positions in the bureaucracy are distributed among the various sects in accordance with strict traditions and regulations.

Sectarian policy has fostered corruption and political interference in the bureaucracy, made the bureaucracy a refuge for unqualified individuals, and weakened internal supervisory controls. A superior may not be able to discipline a subordinate belonging to a different sect, and executives may hesitate to delegate authority for the same reason. In both cases the smooth functioning of administration is obstructed.[11]

In view of its commitment to confessionalism, complete elimination of such orientation in the selection of its bureaucracy seems unlikely, at least in the near future.

    b. *Nepotism:*   Nepotism in Lebanon, as in many developing countries, is related to strong family loyalties. Given the purely traditional perspective that still prevails in Lebanon, it is not only socially permissible, but mandatory that a za'īm appoint members of his immediate and extended family to prestigious posts in the bureaucracy. The qualified son of an ordinary citizen has little chance to win a post when pitted against an equal or less-qualified son of a prominent leader. Although it is no longer possible to appoint sons and cousins to high posts in the administration if these are obviously without qualifications, a qualified system of nepotism continues to prevail, superimposing added constraints and external loyalties on the bureaucracy. A bureaucrat who owes his appointment to confessionalism and nepotism is likely, at the bidding of either patron, to delay, derail, or otherwise obstruct regular administrative procedure. In the 1958 civil conflict, for example, the bureaucracy was paralyzed by the external loyalties of its members to the conflicting za'īms, which led to administrative anarchy. For example, an upper bureaucrat supporting a rebel leader, would refuse to process a transaction desired by a supporter of the government, or even one requested by the government, if he did not have permission from his political patron.

c. *Bribery.* This is not easily defined, since an act of bribery in one culture may be an extension of social niceties in another, providing another source of practical conflict with standards of objectivity and impersonality. While some social scientists[12] rationalize the role of corruption in developing nations, reformers in these nations usually have been dedicated to its elimination. Lebanese, and indeed, Ottoman, experience proves that legislation usually has been an ineffective remedy. In a culture where the peasant is expected to bring his superior a gift (usually a sample of his produce) before he may ask for his *wāsṭah* (intercession), and in which personal elements generally are decisive, the possibility of completely removing bribery —a lubricant familiar to the citizen seeking his way in the unfamiliar bureaucratic situation—is dubious.

The costs of bribery in Lebanon are probably high, in particular when it involves upper bureaucrats taking "cuts" for awarding government contracts or receiving payments for waiving administrative regulations. There can be little question that

90 Modernization Without Revolution

funds badly needed for modernization purposes have been thereby dispersed to other destinations. Indeed, corruption had become so rampant following the investment boom of the 1950s and early 1960s, that the cabinet under the leadership of President Ḥilu and Premier Karāmi, was led in 1966 to undertake the most thorough purge of the upper-level bureaucracy ever attempted.

    d. *Laxity and Influence.* Perhaps the most serious bureaucratic bottleneck to modernization—more so than confessionalism, nepotism, or bribery—has been its spirit of laxity.[13] The Lebanese bureaucrat often comes to work late, shows little interest in his job, goes home early, and takes maximum advantage of loose regulations affecting leaves with pay. Government administrative policy is itself lax, giving twenty-five official and religious holidays and twenty working days vacation for its employees. Working hours, from eight in the morning to two in the afternoon, are shortened further by the hour or so taken by the bureaucrat himself from both ends of the day. The introduction of time clocks in 1959, instead of remedying matters, has resulted in defiance, leading to countless inventions to circumvent their usefulness.

According to a top inspector of the Lebanese bureaucracy, laxity pervades not only the lower echelons of the bureaucracy, but also characterizes its upper levels. "Although they [the top bureaucrats] are expected to be leaders and pacesetters, their behavior does not, in fact, differ from that of their subordinates, except that they sign more documents. They are not unlike postmasters indiscriminately shuffling paper from one official to the other."[14]

The Grand Sérail, a large Ottoman structure which is the main seat of the bureaucracy, offers a good example of these patterns. Situated on an elevated point in the heart of Beirut, it is graced with many arcades, an open inner courtyard, and a magnificent old clock with four faces in front, each face indicating a time different from the others. Winding steps at the entrance lead to an imposing gate, reminiscent of an old castle, appropriately guarded by rifle-carrying gendarmes. Yet to the right of the steps, and in full view of all who enter, lies a heap of junk that has been growing with time, as if it were a reminder of the spirit of ease and lack of concern prevailing within.

On the assumption that bureaucrats must clear their desks before they face the public, no one is allowed into government offices before ten o'clock. Since only a few know of this rule and many citizens from rural areas come to Beirut early so that they can return to their villages before dark, a crowd (never a line) usually forms before the Sérail entrance by 8:30 in the morning. Nevertheless, no one is admitted before ten o'clock, except the influential person who has the proper "style" with the guard, the "operator" who dashes in before he is noticed, the "well-placed" individual whom the guard recognizes and beckons in, those who are noticed by their friends on the inside and are escorted through the gate with triumphant defiance, and those who come armed with personal letters from the za'īms. When at ten the undistinguished are admitted, they are sometimes searched for arms (the more humble the appearance the more thorough the search). Once inside, one discovers that the bulk of the vigorous activity in the long corridors is made by coffee men serving refreshments to the bureaucrats and their guests. The business time of the coffee man generally has a faster tempo and more élan than the bureaucratic time within the offices. While some bureaucrats work conscientiously, the general atmosphere of the bureaucratic offices is one of leisure. Even at the height of business hours—between ten and twelve — a number of bureaucrats leave their offices to visit their colleagues, drink coffee, read the newspaper, or exchange jokes. From twelve until closing time at two, office work tapers off slowly; in many offices it reaches a standstill by one o'clock.

With limitations such as these, the effects on policy can be, and have been severe. The government is inhibited from undertaking programs beyond the bureaucracy's constrained capacity to implement. The public does not look to the government to evolve major programs of development, and efficacy of government intervention to redress socio-economic imbalances through development is impaired, if not undermined. Lebanon's bureaucracy—personalized, confessionalized, and factionalized—is adequate for highly traditional services requiring a minimum of specialization, but not for a modern state such as that demanded by its intellectuals. Political reform is difficult because the political ruling class does not want to introduce changes that might compromise its power. Therefore it attempts to reform the bureaucracy as an alternative. Intellectuals know that the ruling class would rather reform the bureaucracy than itself, and, therefore, realistically expect reforms mostly in the latter. Reforms in the bureaucracy have seemed to some the only viable substitute for reforms in the prevailing political formula, which not only is difficult to change, but has indeed worked adequately in providing political stability.

Reform

Since independence, the za'īms have been expressing their desire to modernize the bureaucracy as a first step in modernizing the new country, but they have had neither the drive nor the know-how to effect important changes. Many reform attempts have been hasty, haphazard, incomplete, and utterly ineffective. In 1952 President Sham'ūn came to office pledging an overhauling of the bureaucracy and each of his successors has made a similar pledge.

The first cabinet formed under Shamʻūn's presidency asked parliament to grant it extraordinary powers for a period of six months to pass legislative decrees that would reorganize the bureaucracy and improve its efficiency. Ninety new laws appertaining to organizational and regulative matters were passed in a few months. These reforms were based on recommendations made by directors and directors general, i.e., by bureaucrats themselves on the basis of individual experiences; they were not based on systematic studies. The shortcomings of these reforms became evident within two years after their application. In 1954 the cabinet of Sāmi al-Ṣulḥ asked and received from parliament extraordinary powers to revise the legislative decrees of 1952.

Realizing the need for expert advice in reforming the bureaucracy, al-Ṣulḥ's government asked the assistance of the Ford Foundation to study the bureaucratic problems and needs of Lebanon and submit recommendations to the prime minister. The resulting report emphasized Lebanon's need for an administrative system shaped to its own needs, stating that the "second-hand administrative machinery inherited from the Turks and the French was not created to be, and is not, effective machinery for carrying out the economic, social, and cultural development programs of a virile young free repulic." It recommended the establishment of a National Civil Service Commission to institute and manage government-wide personnel programs. To instill a professional spirit in the bureaucracy it recommended the establishment of a Society of Public Administration that would bring officials together professionally and expose them through journals, lectures, and seminars to new ideas and methods in administration.

The cabinet accepted the idea of a National Civil Service Commission for personnel management but instituted its own version of such a unit. This was in the form of a Permanent Civil Service Council, which consisted of the director-general of the office of the prime minister as chairman and all other directors-general as members and was to function as an advisory body reporting to the cabinet. However, a council of already-overworked bureaucrats was not what was needed. Subsequent effort of the Ford Foundation to advise the newly established council did not produce the desired results. The slow and ineffectual work of the council came to a virtual standstill after the events of 1958.[15] The Shihāb regime (1958-64), like its predecessor, was also committed to administrative reform and social justice through governmental action. Its first cabinet, headed by Rashīd Karāmi, also sought and received from parliament extraordinary powers for six months to pass legislative decrees intended to overhaul the entire administrative structure. A Central Committee for Administrative Reform, consisting of twenty-four members, was created and attached to the office of the prime minister, ten of whom were high-level bureaucrats and the remainder prominent figures from the private sector. Work committees were assigned to each ministry to study its needs and make recommendations to the Central Committee, which divided its responsibilities among seven subcommittees. Operating at a furious pace and with little expert advice, these committees and subcommittees drafted 162 legislative decrees reorganizing the entire bureaucratic structure. This legislation with all its limitations represents the most extensive reform effort yet undertaken by independent Lebanon.

The resulting reforms, beginning in 1959, have had the support of a number of leading members of the bureaucracy, the continuous advice of consultants, and the President's own commitment to create a modern bureaucratic machine. A new personnel law and the reorganization of the Ministry of General Planning have been basic elements of the changes. In addition, a Civil Service Council to enforce the new personnel law, a Central Inspection Administration and a number of autonomous councils having developmental objectives were also founded.

The Personnel Law of 1959

The Personnel Law of 1959, which is currently in application, classifies government employees as either permanent or temporary and defines the duties and responsibilities of the positions which they occupy. Employees are barred from joining political parties or trade unions, participating in strikes, taking any salaried job other than teaching in schools and universities, and accepting presents or gratuities of any kind. Salaries, extra pay, family allowances, and sickness and death benefits are described in great detail. Promotion is to be only from one rank to that immediately above.

Employees are subject to discipline by their superiors by withholding up to ten days pay or by appearing before a disciplinary council.[16] In 1965 a General Disciplinary Council for Officials was instituted under the office of the prime minister to deal with all infractions except by members of the Civil Service Council, the Central Inspection Administration, judges, security forces, autonomous agencies, and municipalities.

A concluding article of the law states that in all appointments to the bureaucracy, Article 95 of the Constitution, dealing with confessional balance, must be applied. Finally, in the event of a conflict between a ministry and the Civil Service Council concerning application of the Personnel Law, the matter was to be decided by the council of ministers. Thus the confessional base of the bureaucracy was reconfirmed, as was the power of the za'īm class, since the latter usually controls the cabinet.

The Civil Service Council

This was reorganized in 1959 and made responsible for recruitment, promotions, pensions, transfer, discipline, terminations, and related matters for all public officials except judges and members of the security forces. Attached to the office of the prime minister, it consists of three members, a president appointed by decree of the council of ministers, and the heads of the Directorate of Public Officials and Directorate of Training. The Directorate of Public Officials handles all personnel matters authorized by the Council, keeps files on every official, estimates needs for new officials, and conducts all aspects of personnel administration. The Directorate of Training is charged, through its subordinate Institute for Administration and Development, with training officials and preparing new employees to enter the bureaucracy. The Institute conducts training programs for the bureaucracy. So far, though unable to attract academic staff, it has standardized entrance procedures, enforced examination regulations, reduced nepotism, and established concrete criteria for advancement, retirement, pension, and the like. The fact that it does not have full-time academicians specialized in public administration, reduces its effectiveness and its innovative capacity.

Central Inspection Administration

This, too, is attached to the office of the prime minister, its duties being to inspect the entire bureaucracy[17] (with the exception of judges and security forces), for the purpose of punishing those members involved in such irregularities as theft, bribery, negligence; to propose ways and means for the improvement of administrative work; to coordinate work flows; and to undertake studies leading to greater efficiency. For inspection purposes the Lebanese bureaucracy is divided into groups, each of which is responsible to a special Central Inspection service *(maṣlaḥah)*: general administration, engineering, education, health, agriculture, social affairs, finance, and the foreign service. In addition, a Directorate of Research and Orientation and a Directorate of Bidding operate under the Central Inspection Administration. The former, which performs the functions of an organizations-and-methods unit, has been hampered in its efforts by lack of qualified personnel and by the temporary assignment of some of its employees to other organizations.

The fact that most upper-level employees in the Central Inspection Administration are lawyers suggests that it should be more effective in identifying legal infractions than in identifying administrative defects. Its annual reports over the past ten years show that during the average year it adminsters punishment in over a thousand cases, commends good work in about a dozen cases, and issues warnings in about 700 cases. While a great deal can be realized through strict application of law and the threat of punishment, perhaps better results can be achieved through positive action and leadership techniques—areas into which the legally-worded reports of the Central Inspection Administration have not entered.

The Personnel Law of 1959, the Civil Service Council, the Central Inspection Administration, and the General Disciplinary Council represent the four major reform units established during the Shihāb and Ḥilu regimes. These last three bodies are strictly legal in orientation, designed to achieve honest application of the law. Other councils reorganized or introduced under the Shihāb regime which are concerned with the modernization of the bureaucracy deal with tourism, major projects for Beirut, and social development.

Autonomous Bodies

In addition to these administrative units the government has resorted to the establishment of autonomous bodies that would have greater flexibility and greater freedom than the bureaucracies of traditional governmental units and could therefore be more effective in implementing social change. Some of these autonomous organizations, such as the National Council for Tourism, grew out of the individual initiative of Charles Ḥilu, who persuaded President Shihāb to give it official status as an autonomous agency. Only later was it attached to the state administrative machinery. Others emerged in the council of ministers as administrative devices through which the council expected to circumvent existing traditional bureaucracies. The resort to autonomous bodies in Lebanon has been in the upswing for the past decade and is likely to increase with the growth of governmental regulation and control of services. Three such bodies are discussed below as examples.

1. *National Council of Tourism.* The main responsibility for the presently advanced status of tourism has resulted from the efforts of this Council.[18] Its first president was Charles Ḥilu and his successor, Michel al-Khūri, is the son of the late President, Bishārah al-Khūri. Through numerous subcommittees the Council has recommended simplification of administrative processes relating to tourism, encouraged festivals, disseminated information, and organized trips to Lebanon for leading persons from all parts of the world. In many respects

the relationship of the Ministry of Tourism to the National Council of Tourism is that of an administrative agent to a policy-making body. Ḥilu and Khūri have demonstrated the successful role that such councils can perform in supporting the ministries with which they are associated. The success of this council-ministry association has led to a number of proposals purporting the establishment of autonomous councils that would act as spurs to traditional bureaucracies.[19]

2. *The Council for the Execution of Major Projects for the City of Beirut.* City expansion and the rising numbers of development projects have necessitated administrative capabilities going well beyond the traditional municipal structure of Beirut. Introduced by President Shihāb in 1963 to construct and supervise all major projects undertaken in the capital, the Council is governed by a board of three engineers appointed by the council of ministers. As an autonomous body it is neither part of the Municipality nor part of the Ministry of the Interior, although it works closely with both. The cabinet assigns projects to the Council, but once these have been received, the Council can deal directly with the ministries concerned with their execution.

The Council so far has completed the planning and development of a number of municipal areas.[20] It has also been responsible for preparing broad-gauged plans for Beirut, including the building of parks, construction of roads, constructing government buildings in physical proximity to each other to facilitate administrative procedures, and the like.

3. *Office of Social Development.* The Office of Social Development attached to the Ministry of Labor and Social Affairs is governed by a committee of twelve, four of whom are bureaucrats from the Ministries of Social Affairs, Education, and Health and Agriculture, and the remainder prominent private

individuals. Since its institution in 1959 the Office has promoted craft industry and conducted pilot projects in education and public health in especially underdeveloped villages. An impressive center has been built in Beirut to display and sell the products of local industries. The Office conducts studies on various aspects of rural life and city slums and has collected statistics on approximately 50 villages. About 100 of its employees live and work in the villages they are helping.

The above councils afford a new mechanism for resolving crises. They allow a number of people representing divergent views to meet together, iron out differences and reach decisions that, to put it negatively, offend the least number of people. The Council for South Lebanon is such a mechanism.[21]

Approaches to Reform

President Shihāb attempted to reform the bureaucracy by recruiting new men and introducing new bureaucratic and administrative units. He did not attempt to purge the bureaucracy by relieving the inefficient and the unqualified. President Ḥilu, on the other hand, attempted to modernize by thoroughly investigating the upper bureaucrats, terminating the corrupt and inefficient and replacing them with new recruits. Working closely with the cabinet, he requested full powers from the parliament for the cabinet to investigate and replace corrupt bureaucrats. Parliament, in approving the request, in effect authorized the temporary suspension of the law guaranteeing tenure of employment of permanent government employees.

In 1965 the cabinet created an ad hoc unit, al-Hay'ah al-Muwaḥḥadah (the Unified Body), made up of the members of the Civil Service Council and the Central Inspection Administration,[22] to study the bureaucracy and recommend to the cabinet that bureaucrats found to be inefficient, unqualified, and corrupt should be dismissed. Meeting in private sessions under the chairmanship of the president of the Civil Service Council al-Hay'ah had the power of final recommendations. Actions taken under the provisions of the law which established al-Hay'ah and defined its powers were not subject "to any type of revision, not even for the charge of *ultra vires.*"[23] To emphasize further the serious intent of the government, the council of ministers was required to act on the recommendations of al-Hay'ah within ten days after such recommendations were received; failure to act meant the automatic validation of the recommendations.

Bureaucrats who were to be affected by the purge were given a grace period of ten days during which they could resign without prejudice. Fewer than one hundred bureaucrats took advantage of this offer; apparently, the majority doubted the government's intent to proceed. Even the press, which had long favored rigorous reform, was skeptical.

The work of al-Hay'ah was referred to as "the purge," *(al-taṭhīr)* for it purported cleansing the bureaucracy of corrupt officials. By the time the purge ended, about 200 officials had been dismissed, including, to the surprise of most observers, a number of directors-general, ambassadors, and high judges who were close members of the establishment and intimate associates of members of the clubs. The majority was of lower ranks. The government, in an effort to salvage the reputation of the discharged officials, stated its reason for terminating their services to be administrative infraction. In legal terms, therefore, they were neither morally derelict nor criminal and could continue to exercise all their civil rights. On the face of it, no one was terminated for corruption.

The purge was not extensive, but it went perhaps as far as the system could tolerate. It acted as a momentary check on further backsliding. Many zaʿīms, including some serving in the cabinet, were unwilling to assume any responsibility for the purge, placing it entirely on the president. President Ḥilu, unlike perhaps all his predecessors, had been expected to abide by the Constitution and serve only a six-year, non-renewable term. Khūri, Shamʿūn, and Shihāb had strong political or military bases and were all considered likely to put pressure on parliament to amend the Constitution so that they could serve another term in office. A president who has such plans cannot risk increasing his enemies in the clubs by dismissing bureaucrats who may be protégés of prominent club members. Ḥilu had no design on renewal, perhaps because he was not politically strong enough, and he could, therefore, risk alienating a number of leaders, if the returns in terms of administrative efficiency warranted such action. It also follows that Ḥilu was less concerned about aggrieved politicians and religious leaders whose relatives and associates had lost key bureaucratic posts.

After the purge, the President's prestige was clearly enhanced. The press, political parties, trade unions, and social clubs expressed their support for further purges in the bureaucracy. The Council of the Lawyers Syndicate, for example, recommended that more judges should be disciplined or fired.[24]

Because of pressure from zaʿīms who could not afford too much loss of prestige by having their protégés expelled from the bureaucracy, however, the advantage gained by President Ḥilu was not carried through, and the reform drive ended in 1966. The Hay'ah's work was taken on by a General Disciplinary Council, instituted as a new bureaucratic unit with much less power than al-Hay'ah. The Council's operation since 1966 indicates that it can only function at a routine level handling minor infractions, and that it lacks the support and the prestige to discipline high-level bureaucrats or to treat major cases involving corruption.

The failure to follow through in major reforms involving personnel changes is characteristic of a government like that of Lebanon, which is based on a wide consensus and on highly personal relations among the top leaders. A president may wish to replace top bureaucrats but must be careful lest he loses the support of the political patrons of those dismissed bureaucrats.

Reforms under Shihāb and Ḥilu, while not extensive, introduced new bureaucratic units under the leadership of new men committed to modernization. These reforms, far from lowering the prestige of the bureaucracy, have in fact enhanced it. In Lebanon, as in the rest of the Arab East, the bureaucracy has always enjoyed high prestige and been able to attract the educated. If, in the past, the educated elite could not join the bureaucracy without the support of a zaʿīm, the Lebanese reforms since 1959 have opened the door a little wider for educated men and women lacking political backing. In the past decade a handful of these have been recruited on the basis of merit and given responsibilities in finance, inspection, education, and social work.

Improvement of the bureaucracy by recruiting qualified personnel has a fair likelihood of success in Lebanon. Prevailing social values endow bureaucratic positions with high prestige in spite of relatively low pay. Such prestige makes available to the governing class a growing body of educated men who are anxious to be recruited on the basis of merit. Except in a few areas, such as statistics, there is always a greater supply of candidates than the bureaucracy can absorb.

In joining the bureaucracy the candidate becomes *ibn ḥukū-*

mi (literally, son of government), a member of an influential corps, and heir to the historical glories and privileges of a group which once governed virtually as it wished. Entry into the bureaucracy enhances social standing and offers the further opportunity to fulfill a mission, to contribute to national development to a much greater extent than do individuals in universities, schools, or private business.

Summary

Attempts to reform the bureaucracy have been made since independence, and they were intensified during the Shihāb regime. The past decade witnessed the introduction of a new civil service law, new offices, and a growing number of autonomous organizations. Objective criteria in recruitment and promotion have been strengthened, even though they are a long way from replacing traditional considerations. The reforms of the 1950s and 1960s will have to become a built-in, continuing mechanism of government, if bureaucracy is to play a more dynamic role in modernization. The bureaucracy will have to find new linkages with available sources of information and expertise such as universities and research institutes. There will have to be a politically effective consensus that the bureaucracy must play a decisive role in modernization. Not only the za'īms but also members of other clubs—in particular, the ecclesiastic, business, military, and intellectual—must lend their full support to bureaucratic reforms. Such an orientation would necessitate at times sacrificing vested interests and breaking traditional norms.

There is no indication at present that the clubs that determine the governing formula have agreed on thoroughly modernizing the bureaucracy. Indeed, modernization that would disregard confessional, personal, familial, and factional considerations would be extremely difficult. Even the best qualified people hired under Shihāb and Ḥilu were recruited within these constraints.

To sum up, while traditional values prevailing in Lebanon do not, altogether, block modernization, they can slow it and dictate the lines along which it can proceed. The merit system can be tolerated to a certain extent, but it cannot be permitted to encroach on the prerogatives of zaʿīms. Major reforms may be tolerated as relief measures in times of mounting crisis but cannot be tolerated by certain members of the clubs if in conflict with the members' immediate interests.

Lebanon's modernization of the bureaucracy has been a process of conciliation between old and new values, one which has ensured incremental gains for the latter and allowed moderate changes. Such changes have given the bureaucracy a transitional status and indicate that it will perhaps continue to move toward modernization. Today the bureaucracy is very much a reflection of the political formula, most adept at the routine functions commensurate with its preponderantly traditional character. It is clearly more at home in preserving order, accommodating pluralistic interests, and managing—at low speed—the public business of a small polity, than it is in initiating major development projects, providing efficient service to the public, and ensuring a high level of response to growing public demands. The political formula and the transitional bureaucracy are not fully equipped to put into effect a major policy such as development planning. Bureaucrats lack not only the enthusiasm but the techniques to carry out such a policy. Nevertheless, the political formula and the bureaucracy are caught in a process of change entailing continuing modernization.

They both have had to accommodate such changes with varying degrees of success and interest. The following chapter will show how they have entertained the idea of planning and how such an idea has been grafted onto the laissez-faire structure that has prevailed in Lebanon.

V
Planning and Non-Planning: The Lebanese Compromise

Planning is one of the ideas usually associated with modernization that is gaining acceptance in developing countries. It entered Lebanon in a very rudimentary form in the 1930s, and has, since the 1950s, become more conspicuous. The Lebanese government has adopted development planning, as it has adopted bureaucratic reforms, mostly in answer to demands and forces largely outside the strictly formal structure of government and bureaucracy. Believing that the laissez-faire system has been responsible for the relatively prosperous economy of Lebanon, members of the governing class nevertheless are aware that not all Lebanese regions and groups are sharing equally in this prosperity, and therefore that there is special need for government to correct the imbalance. Development planning has been accepted as complementary to laissez-faire in this sense.[1]

In accepting development planning, Lebanon's governing class has proved its flexibility in accommodating change, absorbing the demands of pressure groups, and translating these demands into institutions that may operate under the constraints of all the traditional rules imposed by the political formula. Such acceptance has always been in a manner that would both ensure the continuity of the class in power and deflect the course of such potentially revolutionary groups as disgruntled intellectuals and radicals of the right and left. Development planning as applied in Lebanon may be examined as an aspect of bureaucratic reforms, or as the interjection of new ideas and institutions into the bureaucracy: it is more a technique translated into offices and programs than a basic ideological change. Confessionalism, pluralism, and consensus do not naturally lend themselves to strong central controls no matter how objective or rational these controls may be.

Although development policy is politically expedient, usually it has been applied haphazardly, inconsistently, and at a lower key than has been typical in countries committed to planning. Development planning by its nature tests the ability of the entire political-bureaucratic structure to accommodate change efficiently and on a large scale; thus the Lebanese example shows conflicts between conditions of pre-development planning and its ruling political formula. In short, Lebanese planning has assumed Lebanese characteristics, often hanging between the legal form of planning and sheer anarchy in application.

While Lebanese planning represents a guise under which the governing class may readily effect certain economic and social changes, the amorphousness of the planning process reflects political-bureaucratic mechanisms which operate under polycentric traditional forces—in particular, the confessional constraints limiting national policy formulation. Conversely, the answer to why Lebanon instituted planning, thereby straining its governing apparatus, lies in the readiness of Lebanon's governing class to respond to pressures, to maintain a policy of flexibility that accommodates experimenting with administrative changes, and to draw lessons from political and ideological trends in the Arab East. Its willingness to adopt planning has also been in part a recognition of the unsatisfactory state of uncoordinated development. Under laissez-faire, many were deprived of acceptable employment and educational and health opportunities. Regions, too, have differed greatly in economic and development terms. Such disparities were aggravated by the fact that the poorer regions happened to be primarily Muslim and the richer regions Christian, a situation that could endanger stability and national unity if left unchecked.[2]

Like other developing nations, Lebanon did not adopt planning to remedy internal imbalance only, but also to improve its international status. Planning has become a means for receiving aid from wealthy nations and international organizations and foundations. The need for money and expert advice often accounts for the adoption of planning ideas by countries that neither understand nor believe in them.

The influence of Lebanon's intellectual elite on planning has been and continues to be considerable. While lacking any sophisticated knowledge of planning and method, this group is strongly persuaded of the need for governmental interference to guide and coordinate national activities in what it conceives to be the public interest. Yet, while many have urged the adoption of planning, only a few have attempted any systematic analysis of its scope. The relevant writings on the subject have appeared in the form of normative essays delivered in locally held conferences or published in Arabic journals and newspapers. Planning is discussed as part of reform, economic-development, or social-welfare policies. Among the main contributors have been university graduates who have studied abroad or served in United Nations agencies, as well as a loose association of French-educated intellectuals, known as the Lebanese Society of Political Economy, which flourished in the early independence period. Some of its members were destined to play key roles in planning during the 1950s and 1960s.[3]

Planning ideas gained ground in the early 1950s as part of the general reform movement that led to the resignation of President Bishārah al-Khūri and election of President Shamʿūn in 1952. Khūri's administration had been accused of slowing effective reforms. His opposition rallied to Shamʿūn, who promised major administrative and socio-economic changes and in fact established, after becoming president, a Planning Board (1953) and a Ministry of General Planning (1954). However it was not until the civil conflict of 1958, which was in part a confessional conflict and in part a conflict between the "haves" and "have nots," that planning was taken seriously by President Shihāb as a mechanism for developing the poorer regions of Lebanon and for balancing the economy. President Shihāb was committed to planning and tried to strengthen the planning mechanism by giving it his personal attention. In implementing his planning policy, Shihāb depended on a handful of experts who worked closely with him, almost disregarding the zaʿīms. He depended in particular on Father Louis Joseph Lebret,[4] who was entrusted in 1959 with the task of making a comprehensive survey of Lebanon's resources to provide the empirical data needed for planning purposes. After the survey had been completed in 1960, Father Lebret was asked to submit a development plan for Lebanon and encouraged by the president to advocate— through the use of various media—the egalitarian goals of the Shihāb regime: the desire of the president to introduce professional and scientific techniques in the formulation and implementation of public projects, and the need for cooperation between the private and public sectors.[5] Father Lebret's ideas on planning and administration underlie the eventual orientation of the Ministry of General Planning. The IRFED studies between 1959 and 1964 subsequently became the basis of the 1965 Five-Year Plan.

Although the idea of planning has, in general, been enthusiastically supported by intellectuals and by President Shihāb and his followers, neither its birth as an organizational entity in 1954 nor its reorganization in 1959 was received with wide public interest. No vigorous debate and no major commentaries by the press preceded or followed either event in 1954 or in 1959. Under Sham'ūn and under Shihāb, members of parliament supported it with little interest, however, mainly because it seemed to have the backing of the incumbent president. Za'īms who benefited from a non-interventionist policy were unenthusiastic. As Tinbergen points out, "really fundamental aims cannot be expected of governments or political groups that are inclined towards laissez-faire."[6] The banking community was neutral, either because it believed Lebanon could not seriously undertake planning or because it was concerned with the more important corollary—the Central Bank then being instituted. Nevertheless, a Ministry of Planning was established and was heralded by the Shihāb regime as the agency that would transform Lebanese society and ensure justice and equity to the poorer regions and the lower-income classes.

The law reorganizing the Ministry was written with a great deal of care under the personal scrutiny of President Shihāb. The section below examines the structure of the Ministry as stated in the law and as it operates in practice.

Planning Mechanism

The Ministry of General Planning, reorganized in 1959, is charged with the formulation of broad policies. These policies are to be formulated by various units, as indicated below.

The Planning and Development Board is to prepare a comprehensive development plan. The Directorate of Central Statistics is to be responsible for collecting, analyzing, and publishing statistical data. As the chart shows, the Directorate of Research and Planning represents the core of the Ministry insofar as having immediate contact with projects in process are concerned.

The Development Planning Service is responsible for defining planning goals and national objectives involving levels of standard of living, planning economic infrastructure, and providing urban and rural development programs. Its Economic Research Service conducts studies on employment, social security, housing, social problems, agriculture, industry, commerce, travel, tourism, and finance, based on statistics provided by the Directorate of Central Statistics. The Annual Programs Service plans and supervises projects within the terms of reference laid down by the yearly budgetary cycle, working within the guidelines of the projected five-year plans. The Regional Activities Service works with the governors of the five *muḥāfaẓāts* (administrative regions) to integrate the country through a central planning process.

Although it is neither fully nor adequately staffed, the Directorate of Central Statistics has been able to produce a number of basic studies, as well as to publish a monthly journal of statistics, a quarterly journal of foreign trade, yearly statistical collections, and other ad hoc statistical materials. Its studies have ranged broadly over such subject matter as population, agriculture, industries and crafts, construction, water and electricity, commerce, prices, housing, education, labor force, income distribution, and family income. The Directorate has also been able to overcome the deeply implanted tradition against providing information to the governing authority. Collection of

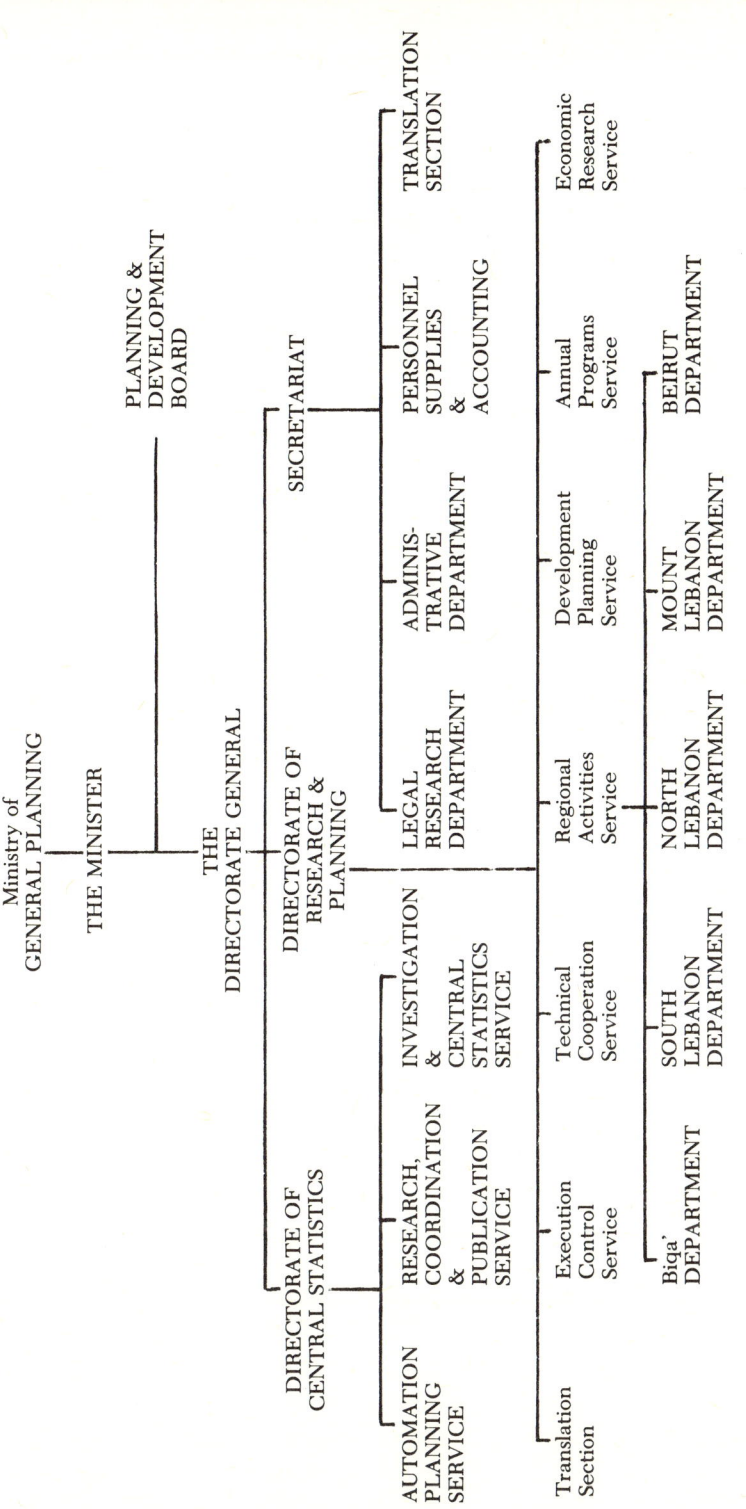

The Planning Mechanism in Lebanon

Ministry of
GENERAL PLANNING

THE MINISTER

PLANNING &
DEVELOPMENT
BOARD

THE
DIRECTORATE GENERAL

SECRETARIAT

DIRECTORATE OF CENTRAL STATISTICS

DIRECTORATE OF RESEARCH & PLANNING

LEGAL RESEARCH DEPARTMENT

ADMINISTRATIVE DEPARTMENT

PERSONNEL, SUPPLIES & ACCOUNTING

TRANSLATION SECTION

AUTOMATION PLANNING SERVICE

RESEARCH, COORDINATION & PUBLICATION SERVICE

INVESTIGATION & CENTRAL STATISTICS SERVICE

- Execution Control Service
- Technical Cooperation Service
- Regional Activities Service
- Development Planning Service
- Annual Programs Service
- Economic Research Service

Translation Section

Biqa' DEPARTMENT

SOUTH LEBANON DEPARTMENT

NORTH LEBANON DEPARTMENT

MOUNT LEBANON DEPARTMENT

BEIRUT DEPARTMENT

Reproduced by permission from George Grassmuck and Kamal Salibi, *Reformed Administration in Lebanon* (Ann Arbor: Center for Near Eastern and North African Studies, University of Michigan; and Beirut: the Department of Political Studies and Public Administration, The American University of Beirut, 1964), p. 79.

data on the activities of individuals is suspect in countries where there has been a tradition of autocratic government. The Lebanese have learned, as an art of survival, not to release information that may be used against them; they tend not to cooperate, or worse, to give the wrong information.

Serving the Ministry of General Planning in a staff capacity is the Planning and Development Board. This consists of ten members appointed by the council of ministers for a period of three years (subject to reappointment) from among those knowledgeable in economics, organization, development and social sciences. The Board is authorized to provide general direction for the preparation of plans and projects, express its opinion on programs submitted to it by the Directorate of Research and Planning, and give advice in respect to instituting adequate financial, economic, social, and development policies.[7]

The Ministry of General Planning works closely with all ministries. The Finance Ministry must authorize expenditures and the Public Works Ministry usually executes approved projects. Furthermore, the plans drawn up by the Ministry of General Planning tend to be groupings of projects submitted by other individual ministries, each of which usually has a number of projects arranged in order of priority and drafted by its top bureaucrats under the auspices of its minister.

A degree of coordination among the projects of the various ministries is achieved in meetings held four times a year attended by the directors-general of all ministries and the Minister of General Planning. These meetings give the directors-general an opportunity to examine their projects vis-à-vis others and make or recommend changes. Once a project is drawn up and agreed upon by both the ministry concerned and the Ministry of General Planning, it is submitted to the Ministry of Finance to determine its financial feasibility. The Ministry of Finance consequently has a substantial share in the planning process.

The role of the Ministry of Finance in the planning process is enhanced by a number of factors. First, the prime minister himself usually occupies this post; when he does not, it is occupied by a Minister who is very close to the president or to the prime minister. Second, the top members of the bureaucracy in the Ministry of Finance are highly trained and experienced officials. Third, since the Ministry of Finance is in charge of budget formulation, it controls the purse strings, the eventual touchstone for plan feasibility and implementation.

Plans

Under this planning mechanism, two plans have been drafted and a third covering the period of President Franjiyyah's tenure in office (1970-76) is gradually unfolding. In both the 1958 and 1965 plans, the role of foreign experts was decisive, though the actual drafting was carried out by the Planning and Development Board in the Ministry of General Planning.

The 1958 plan[8] is important in the history of Lebanese planning because it sums up the reform philosophy of the governing class as expounded in cabinet statements. An underlying welfare orientation pervades the plan, which was conceived in the public interest, to promote social justice and social equality and to mitigate the hardships facing the poorer classes. Employment agencies, social-security measures, and reform of the tax structure to relieve the poorer classes were among the means proposed for the promotion of welfare.

The plan further proposed reform of the government's administrative structure, which it claimed was urgently needed

TABLE 5.1

Estimated Cost of the 1958 Five-Year Plan
(Thousands of Lebanese Pounds)

Types of Projects and Their Classifications	1958	1959	1960	1961	1962	Total
Survey						
1) Land Survey, Demarcation, Unification, and Map Drawing	840	840	840	840	840	4,200
2) Sub-surface Geological Exploration	683	683	683	—	—	2,049
3) Exploration of Water Resources and Planning Their Utilization	392	392	392	125	—	1,301
Total	1,915	1,915	1,915	965	840	7,550
Utilization of Water Resources						
1) Distribution of Drinking Water	14,000	14,000	14,000	14,000	14,000	70,000
2) Irrigation	10,000	10,000	10,000	10,000	10,000	50,000
3) Electrification	31,700	31,700	31,700	31,700	31,700	158,500
Total	55,700	55,700	55,700	55,700	55,700	278,500
Agricultural Projects						
1) Relation between Landowners and Renters	—	—	—	—	—	—
2) Laboratories, Experimental Fields, and Nurseries	645	645	160	160	160	1,770
3) Schools and Guidance	2,423	2,423	208	208	208	5,470
4) Farming Tools and Equipment	250	—	—	—	—	250
5) Seed Stores and Drying and Packing Centers	5,700	5,700	200	200	200	12,000
6) Marketing Cooperatives	—	—	—	—	—	—
7) Forestry Development	862	2,719	2,219	2,219	2,219	10,238
8) Office of Agricultural Economics	70	70	35	35	35	245
9) Exports of Agricultural Products	625	125	125	125	125	1,125
10) Fisheries	950	150	150	150	150	1,550
Total	11,525	11,832	3,097	3,097	3,097	32,648

TABLE 5.1 (continued)

Types of Projects and Their Classification	1958	1959	1960	1961	1962	Total
Industrial Projects						
1) Organization of Industries	200	200	200	200	200	1,000
2) Department for Industrial Economics	52	52	22	22	22	170
3) The Exploration of Industrial Potentialities	270	270	270	270	220	1,300
4) Village Crafts	258	210	210	210	210	1,098
5) Industrial Schools	600	800	1,000	1,200	1,400	5,000
6) The Beirut International Fair	9,400	400	400	400	400	11,000
Total	10,780	1,932	2,102	2,302	2,452	19,568
Tourism and Summer-Vacation Projects						
1) Tourism and Summer Vacation	7,000	7,000	7,000	7,000	7,000	35,000
Projects for the Development of Transportation Network: Ports, Airports, and the Organization of Cities and Villages						
1) The Development of Transportation Networks	25,400	25,400	25,400	25,400	25,400	127,000
2) The Organization of Cities and Villages	21,000	21,000	21,000	21,000	21,000	105,000
3) Ports and Airports	18,000	17,000	12,500	4,000	4,000	55,500
4) Government Buildings	3,426	3,426	3,426	3,426	3,426	17,130
Total	67,826	66,826	62,326	53,826	53,826	304,630
Social Projects						
1) Employment Office	155	135	100	100	100	590
2) Social Security for Workers	625	600	600	600	600	3,025
3) Public Housing	5,000	5,000	5,000	5,000	5,000	25,000
4) Rural Health Services	4,639	4,194	4,194	4,194	4,194	21,415
5) Rural Development Project	6,300	6,300	6,300	6,300	6,300	31,500
6) Schools	4,000	4,000	4,000	4,000	4,000	20,000
Total	20,719	20,229	20,194	20,194	20,194	101,530

TABLE 5.1 (continued)

Types of Projects and Their Classification	1958	1959	1960	1961	1962	Total
Statistical Projects						
1) Departments and Central Bureau of Statistics	1,150	700	700	700	700	3,950
2) Statistical Analysis	300	300	300	300	300	1,500
Total	1,450	1,000	1,000	1,000	1,000	5,450
The Governmental Projects for Money, Banking and Finance						
1) Office of Banking Statistics	50	50	50	50	50	250
2) Central Bank	—	—	—	—	5,000	5,000
3) Legislation to Organize the Banking Profession	40	—	—	—	—	40
4) Office of Monetary and Banking Affairs	50	50	50	50	50	250
5) The Institution of Credit Cooperatives and the Institution of Central Bank for Cooperative Credit	1,250	1,250	1,250	1,250	1,250	6,250
6) Reforming the Tax Structure	200	200	200	200	200	1,000
Total	1,590	1,550	1,550	1,550	6,550	12,790
Project of Customs Policy						
Public Administration Projects						
1) The Study of the Administrative Structure	200	—	—	—	—	200
2) Civil Service Council	150	150	150	150	150	750
3) Institute of Administrative Training	200	200	200	200	200	1,000
4) Reorganization of the (Planning and Development) Board	200	200	200	200	200	1,000
Total	750	550	550	550	550	2,950
GRAND TOTAL:	179,255	168,534	155,434	146,184	151,209	800,616

Source: *Mashrūʿ Khams Sanawāt li al-Inmāʾ al-Iqtiṣādi fī Lubnān* (Five Year Project for Economical Development in Lebanon) (Beirut, Ministry of General Planning, 1958). Arithmetical errors in the original have been corrected.

and should not await broader social reforms of society. To overcome what it labelled the antiquated structure and inadequate personnel of the Lebanese government, it proposed the institution of a personnel law, increased salaries, strict measures against corruption, and a promotion policy based on merit. To supervise these, a Civil Service Council, as is the case in Britain and other countries, and a center to train the national bureaucracy in modern techniques of management were recommended.

An interesting feature of the plan is its criticism of politicians for their neglect of urban problems, holding them responsible for what it labelled inconsistencies and anarchy in the management of city affairs.[9] In accusing the responsible authorities of lack of sympathy towards planning and lack of appreciation of its social and economic implications, the plan reveals, in part, the frustration of the experts in the bureaucracy who had expected more commitment from the political seats of power than these were ready to give.

In the drafting of the 1958 plan, lack of basic information was a continuing obstacle. The experts had to rely on the incomplete prewar studies made by French bureaucrats and by British consultants in the post-independence period, along with more recent estimates made by Lebanese specialists. The need for more complete information was stressed in practically every page of the plan.

By providing concrete facts and examples, the plan called attention to a foremost national problem of need for closer interaction between governmental units, as well as between the public and private sectors. With respect to the public sector, the plan emphasized that there was practically no coordination between the programs of ministries, pointing to past duplications in their respective programs and to losses ensuing from such duplication. It also recommended a series of partnerships between the government and the private sector in various developmental projects; for example, a National Corporation for Water and Electricity was proposed, to have a capital of L.L.100,000,000, 55 percent owned by the government and the remainder by the private sector.

More generally, the development projects constituting the bulk of the plan centered on agricultural, industrial, and water resources and the construction of roads. These were to strengthen the country's economic system and to facilitate investment by the private sector.

Only a few paragraphs dealt with sources of funding. The cost, estimated at about L.L.800,000,000, was to be covered by the national reserve funds, budgetary savings, oil revenues (income from the Trans-Arabian Pipeline Company and the Iraq Petroleum Company), sale of state properties (buildings or land in commercial quarters, to be replaced by others in cheaper areas), higher revenues through tax reforms, and foreign loans (such as from the International Bank For Reconstruction and Development and Kuwait).

In submitting the 1958 plan, the Planning and Development Board expressed regret at what it termed the plan's many deficiencies and the delay encountered before final submission. Deficiencies were attributed to the weak organizational structure of the Board itself, limited funds, and the Board's lack of administrative and financial autonomy. Nevertheless, the Minister of General Planning submitted the document to the prime minister within a month, with the stated hope that it would be adopted by the council of ministers and put into effect immediately.

In the turbulent months of civil conflict that followed, the plan was never discussed by the council of ministers, never adopted, and practically forgotten. Its value derives from being the only extensive statement ever made available on planning needs and ever prepared by the Ministry of General Planning. Furthermore, several of the projects detailed in it were put into effect individually or later combined with other projects.

In its extensive subsequent review of development needs, IRFED used the 1958 plan only as a broad background. Its own development plan, submitted to the Planning and Development Board in 1964, also was not adopted but utilized as the nucleus for another plan drafted in cooperation with various ministries. The end result, revised in 1965 and officially adopted by the council of ministers in April of that year, has become referred to as the "first" five-year plan. Like its 1958 antecedent, it was conceived of as a group of projects intended to promote development and to further the cause of social justice, as described by Premier Rashīd Karāmi in introducing the plan before parliament: "Planning has become a scientific necessity in our age; for this reason the government shall give priority to all development projects and particularly to the Five-Year Plan. It shall carefully supervise these programs and continue to make studies to accommodate the Plan. It shall do its utmost to ensure balanced growth in all economic sectors and to enhance social justice."[10]

Although considerably shorter than the 1958 plan (373 pages), the 1965 document (54 pages) is more specific and detailed. Unlike its predecessor, it neither deals with the background of each project nor details the legislation needed to put it into effect. It is, instead, a brief listing of projects, their costs, and regional distribution. Table 5.2 shows the distribution of projects according to sectors.

The plan starts with a short summary of estimated costs and income to be used in its implementation. It then moves im-

TABLE 5.2
Table of the Development Projects and Their Cost
(1965–1969 Plan)

(Thousands of Lebanese Pounds)

Sectors	1965	1966	1967	1968	1969	Total
Drinking Water	17,200	16,200	7,200	6,200	6,200	53,000
Land Survey	2,100	2,100	2,400	2,100	1,300	10,000
Electricity						
Transmission	5,000	3,000	3,000	2,000	—	13,000
Distribution	5,200	4,800	4,000	3,000	3,000	20,000
Concessions	3,500	3,000	—	—	500	7,000
Total	13,700	10,800	7,000	5,000	3,500	40,000
Civil Organization						
Studies	800	600	200	—	—	1,600
Equipment of centers	2,400	5,000	—	—	—	7,400
Pipes	4,600	3,200	—	—	—	7,800
Contingency	600	600	—	—	—	1,200
Total	8,400	9,400	200	—	—	18,000
River Channels	—	4,000	4,000	6,000	6,000	20,000
Communications						
Roads:						
Highways	3,000	2,000	10,000	12,000	12,000	39,000
International roads	4,700	3,500	3,300	3,500	3,000	18,000
Principal and secondary roads	9,000	6,000	5,000	6,000	6,000	32,000
Village roads	12,500	5,000	3,000	3,000	2,500	26,000
Total	29,200	16,500	21,300	24,500	23,500	115,000

TABLE 5.2 (continued)

Sectors	1965	1966	1967	1968	1969	Total
Railway and Port:						
Beirut Airport	—	3,000	3,000	3,000	3,000	12,000
Center for Air Safety	1,200	1,200	1,200	1,200	200	5,000
Total	1,200	4,200	4,200	4,200	3,200	17,000
Agriculture						
Agriculture education	250	800	860	920	960	3,790
Centers for testing, sorting, and distributing nurseries for fruit-bearing trees	700	260	280	310	350	1,900
Animal breeding	700	900	800	860	940	4,200
Land reclamation	900	600	200	100	—	1,800
Forestry	370	450	530	600	700	2,650
The Green Plan	1,500	1,500	2,000	2,250	2,250	9,500
Lining avenues with trees	250	250	250	250	250	1,250
Combating diseases and harmful insects	800	600	600	600	600	3,200
Economic and statistical studies	160	140	100	100	100	600
Scientific agricultural research	1,600	3,100	3,300	3,400	3,600	15,000
Silk Bureau	260	260	260	260	260	1,300
Fruit Bureau	800	800	800	800	800	4,000
Miscellaneous and contingency	180	160	160	160	140	800
Total	8,470	9,820	10,140	10,610	10,950	49,990
Fishing	120	800	1,000	1,200	1,880	5,000
Irrigation	11,780	8,220	15,000	25,000	25,000	85,000

TABLE 5.2 (continued)

Sectors	1965	1966	1967	1968	1969	Total
Industry						
Studies	—	600	500	500	500	2,100
Centers of technical training	—	350	350	350	350	1,400
Mining	—	200	500	400	400	1,500
Exportation subsidies	—	1,000	1,000	1,500	1,500	5,000
Tripoli International Fair	4,000	3,000	—	—	—	7,000
Total	4,000	5,150	2,350	2,750	2,750	17,000
Tourism						
Encouragement of tourism and model projects	—	1,000	2,000	3,500	3,500	10,000
Expropriation and equipment to institute tourist centers	—	3,000	4,000	4,000	4,000	15,000
Total	—	4,000	6,000	7,500	7,500	25,000
Education						
Elementary and secondary buildings	500	2,000	3,000	3,000	3,500	12,000
Equipment	720	730	750	400	400	3,000
Buildings for secondary education	—	1,000	1,000	1,000	1,000	4,000
Equipment	200	400	400	500	500	2,000
Professional and vocational training	1,650	2,000	2,000	2,000	2,350	10,000
Teacher training	840	260	200	100	100	1,500
Sports and miscellaneous	1,400	1,000	800	700	600	4,500
Total	5,310	7,390	8,150	7,700	8,450	37,000
Antiquities	3,470	3,000	3,000	3,000	3,530	16,000
Scientific research	4,500	5,000	5,000	6,000	6,500	27,000

TABLE 5.2 (continued)

Sectors	1965	1966	1967	1968	1969	Total
Public Health						
Provision of equipment	—	500	1,000	1,000	1,000	3,500
Health equipment	3,000	4,000	9,000	10,000	10,000	36,000
Laboratories	250	1,400	950	1,150	250	4,000
Health services	150	100	100	100	50	500
Total	3,400	6,000	11,050	12,250	11,300	44,000
Social Projects						
Social development	8,000	13,000	14,000	14,000	16,000	65,000
Public housing	1,000	3,000	4,000	6,000	6,000	20,000
Social security	8,000	13,000	13,000	13,000	13,000	60,000
Employment projects	100	200	200	200	300	1,000
Total	17,100	29,200	31,200	33,200	35,300	146,000
Buildings for Public Administration						
Lebanese University	5,000	5,000	—	—	—	10,000
Modern prison	3,500	—	—	—	—	3,500
Modern prisons in Zahlah and Tripoli	1,200	1,200	—	—	—	2,400
Buildings for telephone installations	770	780	—	—	—	1,550
Buildings for security forces	3,860	2,620	—	—	—	6,480
Other buildings	4,500	4,500	4,500	4,570	5,000	23,070
Total	18,830	14,100	4,500	4,570	5,000	47,000
Employee Cooperative	6,000	3,000	2,000	2,000	2,000	15,000
General Total	154,780	158,880	145,690	163,780	163,860	786,990

Source: See *Khuṭṭat al-Tanmiyat al-Khamsiyyat 1965–1969* (Beirut, Ministry of General Planning, 1965). Arithmetical errors in the original have been corrected.

mediately to a tabular presentation (one of dozens listed without attempts at systematic analysis or interpretation), which provides estimates of the annual investment needed by sectors, such as for electrical projects and land surveys. Road building and airport and seaport development are again emphasized, as in 1958. Needs for development of tourism, agriculture, industry, and education are merely indicated by listing projects, along with projects cited for the improvement of public health, public housing, and the social security program. In addition, the plan refers to the need for development of a campus for the Lebanese University, provisions for the construction of new prisons, and new quarters for security forces (army, gendarmes, and police).

A marked difference between the two plans is the emphasis in the first on public-administration reforms, a theme omitted in the latter, presumably because of the bureaucratic reforms previously introduced under Shihāb.

Planning Effectiveness

Evaluation of Lebanese planning to date can focus naturally on three areas: application of projects listed under the 1958 plan, implementation of sections of the 1965 plan, and operation of the Ministry of General Planning over the last decade.

According to a United Nations study, the Lebanese plan of 1965 "is not so much a comprehensive development plan as a programme bringing together a number of government projects aimed at improving the basic infrastructure."[11] The head of the Parliamentary Committee on Planning, Maurice Jumayyil,[12] referring to programs being prepared in the Ministry of General Planning, made a similar point: "I imagine that it [the plan] is a series of programs spread out over the next five years, but not something that could be called a five-year-plan—rather a group of projects whose only connection is that they are all included in the same report."[13]

The nature of Lebanon's "planning" is, in a sense, a reflection of its economic policy. In the opinion of a United Nations expert, a Lebanese "government policy with regard to economic development does not exist, if by policy one means the presence of a coherent and coordinate plan—through legislation or a program of action—which contemplates to bring about changes in the economic variables according to a system of priorities, with a view to reaching higher goals of production and modified composition of products."[14] Lebanese planning has never been intended as an instrument of *étatisme*, but, rather, as an aid to the role of public and private sectors in stimulating growth while keeping competition alive.

Lebanese plans are indicative and focused on the public sector, providing guidelines for projects to be undertaken under the auspices of government. By their nature, such projects are not expected to be undertaken by the private sector, at least not without governmental guarantees. At the same time, the government itself is not bound by the plans. It examines all projects on a yearly basis and makes allocation of funds for project implementation as politically and economically desired. The decision whether or not to allocate expenditures for projects is made by the council of ministers "in accordance with the needs of the country, the public interest, and the financial and technical capabilities of the state."[15] Although aiming at the "creation of conditions conducive to better distribution of national wealth,"[16] essentially it is ideologically silent.

Neither the 1958 nor 1965 plans announced any broad ideological objectives; neither called for a national mobilization of effort. Unlike the plans of Iraq (1965–70), Jordan (1964–70), Kuwait (1966–71), and Syria (1966–70), the 1965 Lebanese plan steers away from ideological commitment and promises of major-scale reform or even change. Where the plans of the neighboring Arab countries emphasize rebuilding of Arab culture or implementing of modern democratic ideals, the Lebanese plan, with the exception of a reference to broad and undefined social-justice goals, avoids any unitary focus, as if it feared that a planning philosophy might arouse suspicions among the delicately balanced confessions.

As in other countries of the Arab East, limited cognizance is taken of external regional considerations. The 1965 plan takes little account of Syria, Iraq, Jordan, and Kuwait, despite the advantage that might accrue to all from their cultural, social, and economic linkages. Although the Common Market experiment in western Europe has been greatly admired and closer cooperation between the small countries involved could lead to substantial economic growth through specialization, exploration of seas, deserts, and oil and mineral reserves, effective steps to international or regional economic unions have not been taken.

Planning as an instrument of modernization only can be as effective as the political leaders permit it to be. Yet only President Shihāb took planning seriously. Under President Ḥilu the planning function lost the fervor it had in the early days of the Shihāb regime; the Ministry became, as was feared, just one more bureaucratic establishment. President Franjiyyah's regime is attempting to strengthen the ministry, but it is too soon to evaluate the change.

The Minister of General Planning is rarely the most important figure in the planning process. Like other ministers, he depends on the president of the republic and on the premier for his continuity in office. Lebanese cabinets generally have been short lived; yet, judging from the variety of men who have assumed the position, no specific criteria have governed the appointments. They may be Christian, Muslim, or Druze; lawyer, engineer, or businessman, with some knowledge or none at all of planning. They may believe in planning as a mechanism of radical reform or may scorn it as irreconcilable with the Lebanese way of doing things. Lacking a power base, the successive ministers of General Planning have had no major impact on the planning process. To be effective, the minister must have the backing of the president, his colleagues in the cabinet, and a dozen directors-general who are closely related to the planning process. Given Lebanon's tradition of governing, plus the atomized and personalized elements pervading the bureaucracy, such backing is not easily obtained.

The director-general of the ministry can provide stability and management, but not leadership. The latter requires effective communication with many clusters of power beyond the administrative structure of the Ministry of General Planning, and for this, a person of cabinet rank is necessary.[17]

The Planning and Development Board, the working core of the Ministry, functions under substantial handicaps. Board members, on the whole, have been too busy with their respective private interests to give Board business any time at all beyond the two-hour weekly session. It is further paralyzed by the belief that its opinion is usually ignored by the cabinet in deference to political considerations. Having little time to do its own research and lacking staff support, the Board tends to rely on private institutes and branches of the bureaucracy to do its studies, which, by their very nature, tend to be uncoordinated and lacking in perspective.

While the budget of the Ministry has increased about six-fold in a twelve-year period (1957–1969), the professional cadre, mostly engineers and some economists, has not yet been completely staffed. Since 1960 the Ministry has often resorted to contractual arrangements with individuals outside the civil service cadre to do research relevant to the planning process. What started as an exception has since become a rule with a resulting loss of efficiency. In 1968 one-fourth of all employees were on a part-time contractual basis.

In drafting its development plans the Ministry needs ramified data. While data compilation has been improving since 1960, it is still inadequate for rigorous planning. The 1965 plan, with projects pooled together with a minimum of coordination and research, reflects the looseness of its data base and the lack of rigor with which such data were treated. For example, the public-housing project was incorporated in the 1965 plan with a minimum of study as to its need or feasibility. Like some other projects, the public-housing project was haltingly begun, then forgotten, and then begun all over again.

Even a small planning staff, if well educated and highly motivated, could be extremely effective if strategically located in the government hierarchy. In this regard, too, planning in Lebanon is handicapped. The Ministry is located on the outskirts of Beirut, well away from important ministries with which it must work closely. Yet, distance is an important factor in communication in Lebanon, where direct personal contact is essential for expediting business. Its limited powers, small staff, and definitely secondary importance relative to Finance, Public Works, and Interior deprive it of the prestige necessary to attract prominent leaders who could spread its influence and strengthen its position.

Similarly outside the government, the Ministry's capacity for offering useful guidelines to private business is also highly limited. Not only is the private sector more extensive and efficient than the public sector, but any attempt on the part of the Ministry to influence the private sector beyond simple regulative procedures would be resisted. The Ministry may encourage certain industries through the use of tax exemptions and by increasing customs duties on competing products. It does not itself set production targets or define investment policies, etc., either by industry or more aggregatively.

So far no plan has been fully implemented. The 1965 plan has been handicapped by a financial crisis that shook the banking community and affected credit in 1965 and 1966. Public funds alloted for development projects had to be diverted to meet such urgent situations as repaying small depositors for their banking losses. While the June War (1967) did not involve Lebanon directly, it adversely affected tourist trade and industrial development. Implementation of projects also has depended on politically delicate choices of priorities, not always made consistently. As one example, while government has invested in the Tripoli International Fair as a measure to appease Tripoli, construction of the requisite highway planned between Tripoli and Beirut has been delayed. As another example, the building of a campus for the Lebanese university was occasioned by a vocal student body threatening disruptive street demonstrations and strikes.

In regard to individual projects, many of the small ones, such as those dealing with drinking water, land survey, and electrical work, are part of the ordinary work of any government and have been undertaken slowly and intermittently since the formation of the Lebanese state. On the other hand, tourism has given impetus to projects dealing with road building, fairs, and antiquities and has been an area in which the the public sector's role has been notable. Investment in road building always has had high priority in Lebanon, not only to facilitate tourism but to satisfy the demands of the sect leaders. Roads connect Beirut with all the major tourist attractions and resorts: the cities of Tyre and Sidon in the south, Ba'albek in the Biqā' valley, Tripoli and the Cedars in the north, and J'īta Cave in the hills near Beirut. Even here, however, there have been substantial miscalculations and mismatches. The scheduled four-lane highway between Beirut and Tyre is only about one-fifth completed, and the Tripoli International Fair will be of little economic value because its completion date will be prior to that of the highway connecting Tripoli with Beirut.

In providing first-rate hotel, restaurant, and recreational facilities, the private sector has contributed greatly to tourism. The government, in addition to support of the private sector or by its own direct investment in tourist facilities, has accelerated its contribution. The building of roads leading to tourist sites throughout the country has been quickened. Local authorities have been encouraged to develop new sites. Other actions encouraging tourism have included subsidies to hotels and permission of duty-free imports of hotel furnishings, construction of camp sites, and maintenance of a free exchange system with indirect subsidies to Arab tourists who receive a preferential rate of exchange.

In agriculture a few projects have had success while the rest have exhibited at best amorphous signs of progress. One of the most successful has been the so-called Green Plan, designed to help the farmer utilize new land, reclaim formerly arable land, build agricultural roads, and undertake reforestation on a major scale. About L.L.70,000,000 have been allocated, covering a ten-year period, and allowing land reclamation loans of up to L.L.10,000 per farmer. Agricultural roads have been built with the cooperation of farmers, who must forego any compensation for land condemned for this purpose. The trees, bushes, and flowers decorating Lebanon's new highways are a testimony to the effectiveness of the model forestation programs started in various parts of the country.

The growing fruit industry has been given financial support for the establishment of cold-storage companies, bonuses to apple farmers, and the provision of new facilities for exporters. In 1967–68 the Fruit Office, located in the Ministry of Agriculture, sought to support apple growers by offering to buy a maximum of 1,000 boxes per farmer at specified prices. Somewhat ironically, the result of this policy was overproduction and a crisis in marketing the fruit abroad.

An example of ventures shared by government and by the private sector—a policy encouraged by the 1958 plan—is the Banque de Credit Agricole. Forty percent of its capital is governmental and the remainder private. By the end of 1968 the Bank had transacted over 12,000 individual loans totalling approximately L.L.103,000,000 and at rates of interest which are low by Lebanese standards (approximately 5.5 percent to farmers and 5 percent to agricultural cooperatives).

Indirect government support has led to wider use of fertilizers and to more modern methods of farming. Government-operated laboratories and model farms provide basic services to those who seek them.

In spite of these positive factors, agriculture in Lebanon remains under strong traditional influences, which impede its efficiency and restrict its productive capacity. Apparently, few farmers know of the possibility of government support and most distrust government. Experimentation on a large scale often involves a certain innovative and risk-taking attitude, as well as sizeable capital, and these are rarely available to the average cultivator. Moreover, while loans from the agricultural bank are possible in principle, actual loans may require a degree of political pull not accessible to everyone.

Although government-research activities, government-operated agricultural schools, and the work of the Faculty of Agriculture at the American University of Beirut (together with its farm in the Biqāʻ Plain) all constitute significant inputs, the capacity of these institutions to reach the farmer has been limited. Observation reveals that such capacity depends on techniques and skills not available to the relatively new governmental and academic bureaucracies in Lebanon.

Some technical-training centers have been established in Beirut and other regions, but these work under heavy social and bureaucratic constraints. Private industry has been encouraged through various types of legislation; to attract foreign capital, for example, industrial plants started since the mid-1960s have been exempted for a limited period[18] from paying income tax. A 1967 law gave further exemptions to new industries located outside Beirut, i.e., in less-developed regions. Immediately after the June War of 1967 and in order to check the economic recession which followed, an Industrial Development Council was formed, under whose influence the cabinet restricted the import of goods produced locally, established government offices to buy and sell locally produced goods, and exempted from taxation raw materials used by Lebanese industry.

Projects stipulated as far back as the 1958 plan, for reforming the tax structure in order to increase state revenue to cover developmental projects, have moved slowly. During Ḥilu's administration, programs for reforming the tax system and providing in-service training for tax assessors were undertaken, but have remained seriously deficient. Because of administrative inefficiency and lack of public cooperation, income from direct taxes is relatively low. Over the centuries the Lebanese have developed a suspicion, not completely unjustified, that the piaster they pay goes into the pocket of a politician or bureaucrat and therefore is better left unpaid. For this reason the government has had to rely largely on income from indirect sources—customs duties and taxes imposed on such commodities as gas, liquor, salt, tobacco, and cement. These affect the rich and poor almost equally, a manifest injustice, yet one which is unavoidable if the bulk of state revenues is to be raised under current conditions.[19]

In the fields of education and social services, the projects listed under the 1965 plan primarily involved school buildings, equipment, training centers, and public housing. Building projects, such as some government buildings, with strong support from influential members of the clubs have been completed. On the other hand, projects purporting modernization of prisons, exploitation of sea resources, and improvement of health facilities in poor regions have moved slowly. With respect to the Lebanese University, listed under "State Buildings," by the fall of 1970 only the science building had been completed while others are still being delayed until future years. Extensive student strikes in 1971–72 in support of rapid execution of reforms in the Lebanese University have led to further promises by the government and to a widening of the chasm between students and political leadership. School buildings, even when constructed under judicious supervision, have been poorly supplied. Equipment supply still lags and, where existent, has not been used efficiently, partly because of inadequate training for instructors and school administrators and also because school teachers and administrators lack responsibility in matters relating to public interest.

As the preceding discussion indicated, it is difficult to determine which projects have been attributable to the institution of planning and which have not. The Planning Ministry's procedure of lumping all types of projects into a five-year plan, with little or no attempt to analyze them or to show their interdependence and objectives, adds to the task.

A number of more general, evaluative conclusions emerge from the foregoing review. Planning seems to have been adopted as a fashionable institution under which projects ordinarily undertaken by a consensus-oriented cabinet can be placed. It thus provides a convenient form which does not hurt and may be of some help. Presumably, separate projects pooled together in a plan are a better guide for decision making than projects that are not so related, while the existence of a body involved with planning has led to the development of a core of top officials who have begun to think in such terms. While the Ministry is itself too weak to make a unique impact on development projects, it has served, nevertheless, as one coordinative unit among many in the formulation of projects. Probably the need for more accurate data has also become clearer as a result of Lebanon's planning experience. Under Shihāb, planning was encouraged personally, but the Ministry lacked the data, experience, personnel, and the extensive political and bureaucratic support needed to be effective. President Ḥilu lacked Shihāb's enthusiasm for planning and did not give the Ministry the support needed to improve its performance. President Franjiyyah has committed himself to revive the ministry and to make planning a focal policy in his administration.

Perhaps above all, the prestige given to the concept of planning by presidential support and the raising of development to an ideology second only to that of national unity, have led the governing class to think more and more in terms of development projects and the reforms needed to ensure implementation. If planning does not function as it should, and if a reformed bureaucracy does not live up to expectations proclaimed by the successive cabinets, then reform cannot be expected to move except at a slow pace and without revolutionary or ideological fervor. If the Ministry of General Planning does not really plan, it nevertheless shares with the za'īms the task of instituting development projects under some sort of a plan.

Limited government is a value shared by za'īms and many members of the clubs who have a special stake in laissez-faire. Established a decade ago, planning seems to have progressed as it was originally intended: to complement the private sector but not to enforce central controls over the economy. To preserve continuity of a polycentric society, variable and sometimes conflicting demands of pressure groups also must be accommodated. In a country in which powerful communities jealously vie with each other, in which a growing bourgeois class requires ever greater and more efficient social services, and in which rising levels of living have become an insistent political force, the need to accommodate change, however amorphically and reluctantly, becomes overriding. So far, at least, Lebanon seems to have found a formula whereby it can perpetuate itself peacefully and entertain modernization ideals in a unique manner.

VI
Prospects for The Communal Society

It has been shown that Lebanon's communal society has established a political formula that can both accommodate change and introduce moderate reforms, provided they do not seriously shake the foundations of the political power structure. The political formula by which it is ruled is determined largely by the za'īms and by the other influential clubs, which have varying degrees of interest in modernization. The za'īms' interest in modernization is highly pragmatic—they want to stay on top and therefore are eager to appease, as much as needed, dissenters and potential trouble-makers. In permitting bureaucratic reforms and a type of development planning, they have sought a more secure environment for themselves under modernization. Accordingly, it has been their option, as decision-makers, to determine the types and amounts of basic development composition, along with the extent of public-private mix: roads, ports, adequate administration, on the one hand; yet, stable economic conditions for the more efficient, enterprising, and hitherto-more-successful private sector, on the other.

Many of the reforms and development projects undertaken by this formula reflect the constraints of confessionalism, factionalism, and personalism. In spite of these constraints, a measure of success has been attained: reforms have been undertaken, some corrupt officials have been relieved of their duties, new men have been recruited, and new administrative units instituted. A planning unit has been established and a plan, embodying a variety of public projects, actually has been formulated and partially executed.

Confessional, communal, and pluralistic Lebanese society has proved, precisely because of its attributes, ability to modernize with little governmental support. In bringing seventeen confessional groupings together, Lebanese society provides opportunities for comparison and encourages competition among them. This competition partially has been responsible for the high premium set on education, professional status, and financial success. Minorities challenged by each other and by the Sunni majority in the Arab East have developed orientations that have proved conducive to modernization. The emigration of Maronites in response to internal Lebanese conflicts in the nineteenth century has proved to be a blessing in disguise for the now highly advanced Maronite community. The Armenian community has responded to its refugee status by developing technical skills and light industries that have, in one generation, earned a respectable and legitimate status in the society.

The Lebanese communal society requires diverse paths to modernization and jealously guards each against the intrusion of a central government that never can represent it fully. A low-keyed approach, following a middle course and depending always on consensus, has been a necessary constraint of the Lebanese formula for rule. Its rulers have four priorities imposed on them by the formula, and it is in this context that their roles as modernizers have evolved. First, they have had to satisfy a large number of agents, represented by the effective leaders of the communities. In dealing with a pluralistic base to accommodate these multiple sources of pressure and power, the za'īms can point to a democratic record, rare in the Arab world and in the broader Afro-Asian context. They have counterbalanced and absorbed peaceful changes of government, adhered to a liberal constitution, and maintained regular popular elections as bases of government. In a region where governmental change and change of regimes are associated with military coups and revolutions, this has been no mean achievement and is the clearest indicator of an evolving modernization among Lebanon's rulers.

Second, the za'īms are expected, according to the political formula, to maintain peace and order and to promote amity and national unity. In an area where the various communities have been fiercely jealous of their autonomy, where suspicions of each other and of central government lie deep, and where political power has been intertwined with religious and confessional loyalties, the degree to which peace and stability have been maintained has been a major achievement, in spite of the civil conflict of 1958. Indeed the 1958 conflict was as much a product of the international forces (Nasserism, the unity between Syria and Egypt, the Baghdad Pact, ideological conflicts among nationalist movements in the Arab East) operating in the region as it was a result of internal forces.

Third, the za'īms have had to defend the prevailing order against outside intrusions. While Lebanon is an Arab country by language, cultural traits, and historical tradition, it is, nevertheless, a special one. Its liberal regime, high level of cultural sophistication, bourgeois style of urban life, and free exchange of ideas pose dangers to neighboring regimes and expose this mercantile republic to threats. Defending a state with a minimal military force against states with far superior power requires wise diplomacy. So far the za'īms have weathered all crises in the region by avoiding them, walking a tight rope, and shielding the country through the Arab League Covenant and the United Nations.

Fourth, the za'īms have sought to ward off civil conflict by heeding the need for social and economic benefits to all communities. Here the za'īms, working within a laissez-faire context and with a transitional bureaucracy, have had only limited success. Their governing formula of moderation has been criticized by intellectuals, radical elites, and, in addition, by some leading za'īms.

The communal society is interested first and foremost in survival, freedom, and peaceful change. Only when these are assured and circumstances permit, does the governing class intervene in the fields of economy, education, and social welfare. In the past, the governing class has entered this area with hesitation, not only because it lacks knowledge and skills in these fields or because its administrative machinery is defective, but also because it has feared that intervention might disrupt its hitherto-successful private enterprise system and thereby its political foundations.

Whether or not the order of these priorities can continue may be questioned. Lebanon's lead in modernization in the Arab World is a result of the momentum it gained from an early start. New ideologies with revolutionary fervor have entered the Arab East in this century, particularly after the establishment of the state of Israel in 1948. The adherents of these ideologies are impatient with incremental reforms and suspicious of liberal regimes whose leaders hail from traditional feudal and wealthy families. These ideologies—nationalism, socialism, communism—have gathered adherents among Lebanese groups and sympathizers among intellectuals and radical elites who question the priority which Lebanon's traditional leaders have placed on peace and stability over development. Many Lebanese ideologists would rather focus on development and the social needs among the poor. Under these conditions, conflict between the za'īms and the radical elite would seem likely.

There is little reason to believe that Lebanon's modernization formula can be made radically more efficient or more interventionist, given the constraints under which it operates. It is also impossible to tell whether interventionism would ensure greater public benefits. The experience of nations in centrally directed planning is still too recent to permit sound judgment on its efficacy.

If the role of the prevailing political formula in modernization has been limited until now, what are its prospects in the future? In other words, what is the prospect for Lebanon's liberal, communal order to continue in the face of mass-oriented, non-liberal, interventionist trends? Four possibilities suggest themselves. First, the present political formula might continue unchanged. Modernization would continue to move ahead, with secondary governmental support in the form of improved administrative machinery and development plans embodying sets of infrastructural projects. Arguments favoring the probability and desirability of this option are based on continuation of the joint communal (za'īm) club political formula that has provided stability in a highly unstable region for more than a quarter of a century. At present few except the radical elite would seek constitutional revision or a revamping of the political system.

Second, there is the possibility of revolution, a weak prospect at present. In the Middle East, political revolutions typically have been led by army officers and no such path to revolution in Lebanon appears likely. No military plot to overthrow the regime and change the political formula is known to have existed, although a few officers joined the attempted coup by the Syrian Social National Party in 1961. The Lebanese army is small and numerically not significantly larger than dedicated followings of za'īms. It is also confessionally balanced. Were a group of officers to lead a revolution, they would probably meet opposition from officers of other groupings. The head of the army traditionally has been a Maronite and, therefore, has most at stake in political continuity. The internecine conflicts that have followed military coups in the Middle East are likely to discourage military attempts at political overthrow in Lebanon. The unprecedented popular elation that followed the victory of Suleiman Franjiyyah in July, 1970, over a candidate who, among others, was supported by the military, was attributed to the desire of the people for a clearly civil government. It was also an indictment of the growing involvement of the military in politics since the civil conflict of 1958.

If, hypothetically, a military coup were to take place and not be defeated by opposing civil forces led by za'īms, its success would be likely to hinder modernization by inhibiting private initiative and discouraging foreign investment. It probably would be frustrated further by built-in constraints in the bureaucracy. The officer might order changes but no one would be forced to take him seriously. This was the experience of a number of revolutionary governments in the Middle East.

The possibility of a popular non-military revolution, led by one or more political parties and involving radical changes in the governing formula is similarly remote. Those most readily available for violence—in the form of revolutions, strikes, demonstrations—are largely under the control of the za'īm class, which has no interest in changing the rules of the game.

As a third possibility, in theory, the president might assume substantially greater powers. Although again this outcome is highly unlikely, support for it sometimes is voiced directly or alluded to by some intellectuals and in newspaper editorials. But the Lebanese system is too complex and atomized for a single leader to leave his mark; were the president to overstep the bounds of power assigned to him by the formula, he would be opposed by the premier, the cabinet, and some or all of the clubs. Radical changes in the inner structure of the formula which might strengthen one sector, policy, or office, while silencing others, are not possible within the existing balance of powers.

If a revolutionary attack against the existing political balance is unlikely to succeed, and if radical changes within the formula are also unlikely, then the conclusion is clear. A fourth possibility, that future modernization involving the public must occur within the prevailing political structure, becomes the most probable one, although the prevailing structure may have to operate under pressures similar to those of 1958. Reforms that would more seriously commit the regime to development and to a widened welfare orientation, would still seem possible, in a context of greater flexibility of approach and objectives by groups continuing to rule by consensus and compromise. Although the za'īms exercise predominant power, they have not been alone in the governing mechanism and their traditional linkages have not necessarily been constraints against modernization. Lebanese political traditions have been flexible enough to permit the za'īms to co-opt competent and educated men from all classes, even from the lower middle class, which so far has had no significant representation in the political formula.

The bureaucracy is another area in which significant change can be made without radically affecting the political rules of the game. For a country in which political options are restricted by a multiplicity of subnational loyalties, the bureaucracy ranks high as a possible agent of change, even after allowing for the confessional constraints which govern it. The reforms of the Shihāb and Ḥilu regimes could have been more extensive and more frequent; and Lebanon, unlike many developing countries, has enough eligible candidates to allow equitable representation of the confessions in a reformed bureaucracy. With the aid of an improved bureaucracy, Lebanese modernization could help redress social, economic, and cultural imbalances between confessions and regions, provided it is given full support by the president and his council of ministers. This should also entail the more direct and continuing linkages between the government and the universities and research centers at home, as well as learned, technically skilled Lebanese in the "intellectual diaspora" abroad. These goals are within the reach of the za'īms and other clubs, without whose active efforts implementation of the modernization ideals held by Lebanese intellectuals cannot be fully attained.

Barring a major political crisis in the Middle East that might affect Lebanon and squander the gains it has achieved over the past two centuries through private effort and limited governmental support, future modernization is likely to continue at a steady, incremental pace. But modernization may be speeded by extensive reforms within the confines of the present political formula and the existing administrative mechanism. Destroying the formula altogether would open a Pandora's box whose potential for good or evil is unknown. Neither alternative can be predicted with a degree of accuracy that would justify taking the risk.

Notes

Introduction

1. One of the most important forums is the *Cénacle Libanais*, a literary club founded by Michel Asmar and partially supported by government subsidy. For over two decades the *Cénacle* has provided Lebanese intellectuals with the opportunity to analyze Lebanese society and construct models for its development. A large number of books and booklets have been issued by the *Cénacle* on various aspects of Lebanon's modernization.

2. For representative ideas on this subject see René Habachi, *Hadāratuna 'ala al-Muftaraq* (Our Civilization at the Crossroads) (Beirut: *Cénacle Libanais* Publication, 1960). Note the lecture series on the administrative, political, economic, and social aspects of Lebanon published by the *Cénacle* in 1965 under the heading *Lubnān* (Lebanon) 1964–1965, and the self-appraisal essays published in 1968.

Chapter I: Forces for Change

1. On the role of the Maronites in the rise of modern Lebanon, see Pierre Dib, *L'Eglise Maronite*, 2 vols. (Paris: Librairie Letouzey et Ané, 1930); Albert Hourani, *Minorities in the Arab World*, (London: Oxford University Press, 1947); Niqula Murad, *Notice Historique sur l'Origine de la Nation Maronite et sur les Rapports avec la France, sur la Nation Druze et sur les Diverses Populations du Mont Liban* (Paris: le Clère, 1944); B. Poujoulat, *La Verité sur la Syrie et sur l'Expedition Française* (Paris:

Gaume Frères et J. Duprey, 1861); Pierre Raphael, *Le Rôle du Collège Maronite Romain dans l'Orientalisme aux XVIIe et XVIIIe Siècles* (The Catholic Press, Université Saint Joseph de Beyrouth. Publication du 75e anniversaire 1950); René Ristelhueber, *Les Traditions Françaises au Liban* (Paris: Félix Alcan, 1918).

2. See William Polk, *The Opening of South Lebanon 1788–1840: A Study of the Impact of the West on the Middle East* (Cambridge: Harvard University Press, 1963), p. XIX.

3. It was issued under British pressure to signal the Sultan's desire to modernize Ottoman institutions and liberalize Ottoman policy towards the subject communities of the Empire. Its aim was to weaken Russia's claim at the Congress of Paris to the effect that the Sultan's Greek Orthodox subjects needed Russian protection.

4. See Roderic Davison, *Reform in the Ottoman Empire 1856–1876* (Princeton: Princeton University Press, 1963). For text of the Hatti Sharif of Gulhane and of the Hatti-Humayun, see J. Hurewitz (comp. and ed.), *Diplomacy in the Near and Middle East: A Documentary Record: 1535–1914*, 2 vols. (Princeton: D. Van Nostrand Co., 1956).

5. Kamal Salibi, *The Modern History of Lebanon* (London: Weidenfeld and Nicholson, Ltd., 1965).

6. The following excerpts are from the cabinet statement submitted by Premier Riyāḍ al-Ṣulḥ to parliament on October 7, 1943: "This government is created by the will of the people. It recognizes no other source for its authority; and seeks no objective other than that of the people. . . . Unless the hearts of all the people rally to the nation, a nation cannot long endure. . . . Our first objective then is to rally the hearts of all the Lebanese to the love of their country; and we know that of paramount importance is our duty to strengthen the foundations of national dignity and pride through appropriate legislations, behavior, deeds and practices. . . . Confessionalism has

often served to promote special interests and worked against the national interest. . . . The moment when confessionalism is eliminated is a moment of blessed national awakening. . . ."

7. Of these, 39 are in Arabic, four in French, two in English and four in Armenian. Zahi Khuri, "The Lebanese Press," *Middle East Forum*, XXXVIII (February, 1962), p. 11.

8. Bruce Russet et al. (ed.), *World Handbook of Political and Social Indicators*, henceforth referred to as Russet, *World Handbook* (New Haven: Yale University Press, 1964), pp. 108–110.

Daily Newspaper Circulation per 1,000 Population

Rank	Country	Circulation per 1,000 pop.	Year
1	United Kingdom	506.	1961
13	United States of America	326.	1960
23	Israel	210.	1957
41	Lebanon	97.	1959
79.5	Egypt	20.	1958
82.5	Jordan	18.	1960
125	Upper Volta	0.1	1957

9. As this table shows, in a listing of 104 countries, Lebanon ranks only after Hong Kong in movie attendance.

Cinema Attendance per Capita

Rank	Country	Cinema Attendance per capita	Year
1	Hong Kong	22.8	1959
2	Lebanon	22.5	1960
4	Israel	18.5	1959
19	U.S.A.	11.8	1961
69	Egypt	2.6	1961
104	Laos	.04	1959

Source: Russet, *World Handbook*, pp. 129–131, for 104 countries.

10. See Iskandar Bashir, *Planned Administrative Change in Lebanon*, (Beirut: American University of Beirut, n.d.), pp. 144 ff.

11. IRFED stands for L'Institut International de Recherche et Formation en Vue du Développement Intégral et Harmonisé de Paris. The mission did its work in Lebanon between 1959 and 1964 under the direction of Father Louis Joseph Lebret.

12. The role of Lebanese entrepreneurs has been investigated by Yusif Sayigh, *Entrepreneurs of Lebanon* (Cambridge: Harvard University Press, 1962). This study shows the extensive activity of these entrepreneurs and their broad cultural contacts.

Chapter II: The Communal Society

1. After the civil conflict of 1958, appointments into the bureaucracy were made on the basis of 6 to 6. Parliamentary representation, however, continues on the basis of 6 to 5.

2. Some projections, particularly those of IRFED, have been very conservative; thus the IRFED projection for 1975 was 2,351,000, a number surpassed in the mid-1960s. An estimate by the Doxiadis group for 1956 was 1,445,000; an IRFED estimate for 1959 was 1,626,000. For population studies of Lebanon see Alexander Gibb et al., *The Economic Development of Lebanon* (London, 1948); IRFED, *Besoins et Possibilités de Développement du Liban*, 2 vols. (Beirut: Ministry of General Planning, 1960–1961); Claude Mazure, *Démographie—Liban et Perspective* (Beirut: Ministry of General Planning, June 1964).

3. Based on the United Nations' *Demographic Yearbook*, 1970. It should be pointed out, however, that existing estimates of population distribution by age (or even sex and province) in many of these countries are not reliable. The United Nations'

Demographic Yearbook leaves many an index of Lebanon's population empty for lack of reliable information.

4. Some estimates of Lebanese population are as follows:

Year	Number	Source
1932	793,426	Census of 1932
1944	1,064,186	Food Office
1945	1,146,793	Ministry of Economy
1956	1,445,000	Doxiadis
1959	1,626,000	IRFED
1962	2,225,000	U.N. *Demographic Yearbook*, 1967
1967	2,520,000	U.N. *Demographic Yearbook*, 1967
1970	2,787,000	U.N. *Demographic Yearbook*, 1970

5. 1 sq. mile = 2.589988 sq. km.

6. The United Arab Republic would be the most densely populated country in the Afro-Asian world, if the habitable stretch along the Nile were the only basis used for computing density.

7. See Food and Agriculture Organization, *The State of Food and Agriculture, 1970*, p. 255. According to the Ministry of Public Health, for 1966 the total number of reported tuberculosis cases was 138; diphtheria 100; bilharzias 5; of all other diseases, including scarlet fever, leprosy, and rabies, only 10 were reported. An exception must be made for 1970, in which about 20 cholera cases were reported.

8. Available data misstate the actual situation to an extent, since many doctors registered in Lebanon actually practice in Kuwait, Bahrain, Saudi Arabia, or Libya.

Country	Inhabitants per Physician	Year
Ethiopia	71,790	1969
Iraq	3,830	1967
Syria	3,880	1969
Egypt	14,830	1969
Lebanon	1,230	1967
Kuwait	830	1969

Country	Inhabitants per Physician	Year
U.S.A.	650	1967
U.S.S.R.	433	1969
Israel	410	1969

9. Source: *Statistical Yearbook*, 1970, Table 200. The Ministry of Public Health reports that the percentage of hospital occupancy for 1966 was about 60 percent in all hospitals, averaging about 75 percent in government-operated hospitals and 45 percent in private hospitals. Hospitalization is expensive in private hospitals but free or at nominal cost in the government-owned or supported hospitals. The high cost of private medical treatment is tempered by the fact that many physicians, for sociocultural reasons, often treat free of charge members of their extended family, friends of the family, and the poor people who attach themselves to their family. In such cases the physician is expected either to give medicine to the poor who depend on him or to offer them money with which to purchase medicine. There are about 550 dentists, of whom about one-third have excellent clinical facilities. The dentists are graduates of the School of Dentistry of the Saint Joseph University in Beirut or of the national universities in Syria and Cairo. Many of them have done post-graduate work in Europe or in the United States. Folk medicine still has a tenacious hold in the rural regions and in the poorer sections of the cities. Such medicine, however, is usually resorted to only in minor sicknesses and is frequently applied in conjunction with modern medicine.

10. Judgments on these scores, it should be noted, must be made from direct observation. It would be difficult to impossible to find written "sources" for this information.

11. Philip Hitti, *Lebanon in History* (London: Macmillan and Co., Ltd., 1957); Albert Hourani, *Syria and Lebanon: A Political Essay* (London: Oxford University Press, 1954); Carleton Stevens Coon, *Caravan* (New York: Henry Holt and Co., Inc., 1951).

12. The history of the confessional, ethnic or "historical" communities has been discussed by Albert Hourani in *Minorities in the Arab World;* see also Philip Hitti, *Lebanon in History;* Wilhelm Kewenig, *Die Koexistenz der Religionsgemeinschaften im Libanon* (Berlin, De Gruyter, 1965).

13. Over 90 percent of the Arabic speaking peoples are Muslims and about 90 percent of the Muslims are Sunnis (Orthodox Muslims), the other being mostly Shī'īs.

14. On the Druze, see Philip Hitti, *The Origins of the Druze People and Religion* (New York: Columbia University Press, 1928); Marshall G. S. Hodgson, "Al-Darazi and Hamza in the Origin of the Druze Religion," *Journal of the American Oriental Society* LXXXII (Mar. 15, 1962): No. 1.

15. No one community, however, is exclusively confined to its region. The Maronites, for example, constitute 90 percent of the *qaḍā'* (district) of Zgharta; 85 percent of the *qaḍā'* of Kisirawān, and 76 percent of the *qaḍā'* of Batrūn, while in the other areas they are a minority constituting 28 percent of the *qaḍā'* of al-Kūrah, 18 percent of the *qaḍā'* of 'Akkār, and 5 percent of the city of Tripoli. In the muḥāfazah (province) of South Lebanon they constitute between 3 and 10 percent of each *qaḍā'*. In varying degrees, the same is true of the other ethnic communities. (I am indebted to Professor Fuad Khuri of the Department of Sociology at the American University of Beirut for his permission to use these figures from his unpublished work on Lebanese confessions.)

16. Arnold Toynbee, *A Study of History*, 12 vols. second edition (London: Oxford University Press, 1934–61), Vol. II, p. 56.

17. Harry Eckstein and David Apter, eds. *Comparative Politics: A Reader* (New York: Free Press of Glencoe, 1963), p. 652.

18. "Ethnicity," in the opinion of Glazer and Moynihan, speaking of the United States, "is more than an influence on events; it is commonly the source of events. Social and political institutions do not merely respond to ethnic interests; a great

number of institutions exist for the specific purpose of serving ethnic interests. This in turn tends to perpetuate them." Nathan Glazer and Daniel Moynihan, *Beyond the Melting Pot* (Cambridge: Massachusetts Institute of Technology Press, 1964 printing) p. 310. On the influence of ethnic groups in another country see Myron Weiner, *The Politics of Scarcity: Public Pressure and Political Response in India* (Chicago: University of Chicago Press, 1962).

19. At present Shī'ī Muslims from south Lebanon are emigrating in growing numbers to Australia. This wave of emigration is due to increasing tensions on the Lebanon-Israel frontier.

20. "There is a general belief in Lebanon that a person, educated or uneducated, can only improve his position by emigration, not by rebelling against working conditions in the country. The belief that emigration improves a man's position is demonstrated by the many Lebanese who have made their wealth abroad, and is reinforced by the fact that among the many emigrants who live outside Lebanon only the wealthy willingly return to the country, either for a short visit or permanently." Fuad Khuri, "The Changing Class Structure in Lebanon," *The Middle East Journal* XXIII (Winter, 1969): No. 1, p. 33.

21. Tribal life such as in Saudi Arabia, Yemen, and Libya is practically nonexistent in Lebanon. A few tribal groups in Lebanon continue to follow the Bedouin code of behavior, but these, too, live a settled life.

22. For life in a Lebanese village see John Gulick, "The Lebanese Village: An Introduction," *American Anthropologist*, Vol. LV, 1953; *Social Structure and Culture Change in a Lebanese Village* (New York: Wenner-Gren, Viking Fund Publication in Anthropology, No. 21, 1955); Afif Tannous, "The Village in the National Life of Lebanon," *Middle East Journal* III (April 1949); Anne Fuller, *Buarij, Portrait of a Lebanese Muslim Village* (Cambridge: Harvard University Press, 1961); Elie Salem, "Local Elections in Lebanon," *Mid West Journal of Political Science*

Vol. IX (November 1965); See also the two articles on "Kafr 'Arz" written by Na'īm 'Atīyyah in *Al-Abhath* (American University of Beirut publication) March and September issues of 1964.

23. Many of the housing projects in the suburbs of Beirut also tend to show confessional contours, although these are much less pronounced than in the villages.

24. As "groups villagers drove away tax collectors during extended periods of modern history." Polk, *The Opening of South Lebanon*, p. 8.

25. An educated person employed in Beirut and Tripoli may often prefer to maintain his home in the village. Many of Beirut's inhabitants maintain two homes—one in the city, the other a weekend home in the village.

26. On attitudes of Christians and Muslims toward change, see Edwin T. Prothro, *Child Rearing in Lebanon* (Cambridge: Harvard University Press, 1961), p. 48 ff.

27. Some villages near the seashore actually own other villages in the mountains, as is the case with Zgharta and Ehden, two villages east of Tripoli.

28. The definition of "urban" varies from one country to another. Denmark may grant urban status to a community of 200 inhabitants. Australia sets a minimum of 5,000. Lebanon's urban population would be a little above 40 percent if a 20,000 population base were taken as a benchmark. This is the figure generally followed by the United Nations in determining urban-rural status.

29. See John Gulick, *Tripoli, A Modern Arab City* (Cambridge: Harvard University Press, 1967) and also his "Old Values and New Institutions in a Lebanese Arab City," in *Human Organization* XXIV (Spring, 1965): No. 1.

30. Some corresponding percentages, given by the United Nations *Demographic Yearbook*, 1970 are: Africa (10), Asia (17), Latin America (27), or for the world as a whole (23). Throughout

the Arab East the capital city is the largest and most important center economically and culturally. In recent years, Baghdad has been found to contain 20 percent of the population of Iraq, Amman 14 percent of that of Jordan, and the city of Kuwait 75 percent of that country.

31. In 1965 the unions succeeded in persuading Parliament to pass a law allowing for the construction of 4,000 units. Work on this project started in 1967 but is presently at a standstill. It is not unusual in Lebanon to begin a project and then stop abruptly, never to start again. The original reason for stopping work may be lack of funds or their dispersal for a contingent development. Once stopped, a project may need as much prodding to start it moving again as was originally required for its initiation. In the spring of 1972 a cabinet was formed including a Minister of State for Housing. It is expected now that housing projects will move at a greater speed.

32. Urban studies in Lebanon are in their infancy. Existing published material is out-of-date and incomplete. Charles Churchill, *The City of Beirut: A Socio-Economic Survey* (Beirut: Dār el-Kitab, 1954); Halim Abu-Izzeddin (ed.), *Lebanon and Its Provinces* (Beirut: Khayats, 1963). Members of the Department of Sociology at the American University of Beirut are currently conducting intensive research on urban patterns in Beirut. On other Middle Eastern cities see Nicola Ziadeh, *Mudun ʿArabiyyah* (Arab Cities) (Beirut: Dār al-Ṭalīʿah, 1965); Jane Hacker, *Modern Amman* (North Carolina: Durham University, Department of Geography, 1960); William Fox, "The Westernization of an Islamic City: Baghdad" Berkeley, University of California, Ph.D. thesis in progress.

33. Other foreign countries—namely, Germany and Italy—sponsor in addition a number of high-level cultural institutes.

34. On higher education and science training in Lebanon see Fahim I. Qubain, *Education and Science in the Arab World* (Baltimore: Johns Hopkins Press, 1966), pp. 345–415.

35. On the history of the university see Daniel Bliss, *The Reminiscences of Daniel Bliss* (New York: Fleming H. Revell & Co., 1920); Stephen Penrose, *That They May Have Life; The Story of the American University of Beirut 1866–1941* (Beirut, 1970 edition); Bayard Dodge, *The American University of Beirut* (Beirut: Khayat, 1958).

36. These are Physics, Chemistry, History, and Arabic.

37. The University is open to all without discrimination, but its Catholic character and purpose have naturally been especially attractive to Catholics; Maronites consider it their own university.

38. Total enrollment for 1966–67 was 2,494, of whom one-half were registered in law. Eighty-six percent of the students were Lebanese, compared to forty-two percent at the American University of Beirut for that year. Lebanese student enrollment at the American University of Beirut reached 52% for the academic year 1972–73.

39. Educational statistics for 1968–69 published by the Office of Statistics in the Ministry of Education.

40. This is specified in the Constitution, Article 10: "Freedom of education is guaranteed, provided it does not conflict with public order and morality, or offend the dignity of any of the religions or sects. The right of the sects to operate their own schools shall not be interfered with in any way, provided they comply with the educational laws issued by the state."

41. Figures based on data provided by the Ministry of General Planning.

42. Two-thirds of the world's population live in countries with a G.N.P. per capita of less than $300 per year. See United Nations, *Statistical Yearbook*, 1970, Tables 180 and 186.

43. In the case of Libya the wealth is still too "new" to have been adequately channeled to the majority of the people, most of whom still lead a poor, traditional existence. The military regime of Colonel Qazzāfi is committed to extensive development, but it is too soon to evaluate the effective implementation

of this commitment. Kuwait's per capita income is also higher than that of Sweden, Switzerland, and Canada and only lower than that of the United States, but again, very unevenly distributed.

44.
Domestic Product in Lebanon
(Based on averages calculated between the years 1964 and 1968. Ministry of Finance)

Sector	Percentage of Domestic Product
Agriculture	12
Industry	13
Hydro-electric output	3
Construction	6
Transport and communication	8
Rent and lodging	7
Banking and insurance	4
Commerce and trade	33
Government services	8
Other services	6
Total	100

45. I am particularly indebted to the Ministries of Finance, General Planning, Economy, and Agriculture for putting at my disposal data which have helped document this section.

46. For a study of the guild see Bernard Lewis, "The Islamic Guilds," *Economic History Review* VIII (1937): pp. 20–37. See also Bayard Dodge, *Muslim Education in Medieval Times* (Washington, D. C.: The Middle East Institute, 1962).

47. On the industry of Lebanon see Mustapha Nusūli, *Nahwa Mustaqbalin Afḍal li al-Ṣinā 'ah al-Lubnāniyyah* (Toward a Better Future for Lebanese Industry) (Beirut: 1968).

48. See George Mudawwar, *Mizān al-Mudfū 'āt al-Lubnāni*, (Lebanese Balance of Payments for the years 1964 and 1965) (Beirut: American University of Beirut, n.d.).

49. In industrialized countries, the percentage of labor force in agriculture is much lower, being about 5 percent in England, 10 percent in the United States, and 15 percent in Israel. See Russet, *World Handbook*, p. 177.

50. A *waqf* is generally operated by a church or a mosque,

the land usually being granted in perpetuity to these institutions. Lack of care or responsibility often leaves such land in a state of disrepair.

51. This of course excludes illegal crops such as hashish.

52. John Brewster, "Traditional Social Structures as Barriers to Change." In *Agricultural Development and Economic Growth*, second printing, ed. by Herman Southworth and Bruce Johnston (Ithaca: Cornell University Press, 1967), p. 66.

Chapter III: Lebanon's Political Formula

1. Feudalism in the strict sense ended in Lebanon in the nineteenth century; however many of the vestiges of feudalism —extensive socio-political controls by the landlord over the peasants working his land, personal dependence of the followers on the landlord and the like—still exist. The Arabic term *iqṭaʿ* (feudalism) is commonly used in Lebanon to refer to the few influential leaders in the rural regions of Lebanon.

2. The mutaṣarrifiyyah regime of Mount Lebanon introduced an administrative council in the 1860s made up of representatives of all major confessions, which had the effect of legitimizing the traditional practice of attempting agreement among the communities before decisions were made.

3. For detailed study of Lebanon's political process see Pierre Rondot, *Les Institutions Politique du Liban* (Paris: Institute d'Étude de L'Orient Contemperain, 1947); Charles Rizk, *Le Régime Politique Libanais* (Paris, 1966); Michael Hudson, *The Precarious Republic* (New York: Random House, Inc., 1968); Leonard Binder (ed.), *Politics in Lebanon* (New York: John Wiley & Sons, Inc., 1966). On the Pact see Kamāl al-Ḥajj, *Falsafat al-Mīthaq al-Waṭanī* (The Philosophy of the National Pact), (Beirut: 1961); Emile Bustāni, *Al-Mīthaq al-Waṭani wa-*

Mustaqbal Lubnān (The National Pact and the Future of Lebanon) (Beirut n.d.).

4. The first cabinet statement of independent Lebanon read: "Lebanon shall not be a seat for imperialism nor a bridge bringing imperialism to its sister Arab states." Every attempt to tamper with this formula has led to political conflict. The civil disorder of 1958 was attributed in part to the Western orientation of the last government formed under President Shamʿūn. That orientation was deemed to be in conflict with the "neutralist" orientation that was developing in the rest of the Arab world during the 1950s. The mutual renunciation of external "flirting," the one with "Western Christendom" and the other with "Sunni Arabism," was a sort of reassurance that independence was not a "step" leading to the realization of the aims of one group at the expense of the other.

5. Professor Michael Hudson in a study on the parliamentary elections of 1960 found candidate's expenses ranging from $6,600 to $226,000. He estimated the per capita campaign cost for Lebanon in 1960 to be around $1.78 as compared with $.90 for the United States, $.50 for Italy, $.25 for West Germany. *The Electoral Process and Political Development in Lebanon* (Reprint Series, Research Center in Comparative Politics and Administration, Brooklyn College of the City University of New York), No. 3. P. 180.

6. Let's say in district "x" the law assigns three parliamentary seats—two for the Shīʿīs and one for the Maronites, in accordance with the numerical confessional structure in that district. The Shīʿī zaʿīm in that district is virtually assured of victory because of the stature of his family and the pervasive economic, political, and social controls which he holds over his followers. The other Shīʿī and Maronite seats in that district can usually be gained only by those candidates who run with the zaʿīm on the same ticket. A high price is exacted in cash for the privilege of being included on that ticket. As many candidates may run for

election as are eligible and who can afford the deposit, but the chances of success for those who do not have wealth or za'īm support are low.

7. See Samir Khalaf, "Primordial Ties and Politics in Lebanon," *Middle Eastern Studies*, (April 1968).

8. Hudson, "The Electoral Process and Political Development in Lebanon."

9. For a detailed look at the election of the president, see *Mulhaq al-Nahār* (al-Nahār supplement), December 25, 1969.

10. One notable exception to this practice has been the election of the incumbent Suleiman Franjiyyah, whose candidacy was strongly contested by Eliyas Sarkīs, the head of the Central Bank and the candidate of ex-president Shihāb and his following in parliament, known as *al-Nahj al-Shihābi* (i.e. Shihāb: Method or Direction). Franjiyyah won by one vote on the third ballot.

11. See Bishārah al-Khūri, *Haqā'iq Lubnāniyyah* (Lebanese Truths), 3 vols. (Beirut, 1961), in passim.

12. There are no more than about half a dozen Muslim leaders who are serious candidates for this office at any one time. Lebanese premiers generally come from Beirut and Tripoli, and are usually members of wealthy families who have been socially and politically prominent since the Ottoman period.

13. The one exception was the Minister of Education and Information, Ghassān Tweini, editor of *Al-Nahar* newspaper and former member of parliament. After a few months Tweini resigned and was replaced by a non-political figure, a professor of medicine.

14. The writings of intellectuals on this subject have been mainly in the following journals: *Mawaqif, Dirasat 'Arabiyyah, al-Adīb, Mulhaq al-Nahār, al-Usbū' al-'Arabi,* and in *L'Orient* newspaper. The publications of the *Cénacle Libanais* and of the

Institute of Developmental Studies also provide extensive material on this subject.

15. Including the Karāmis, Shihābs, Salāms, As'ads, Junblāts, Eddehs, Khūris, Sulhs, and Ḥimādahs.

16. Historically, armies in the Arab world have always been directly involved in politics. Generals have been enthroning and dethroning Islamic heads of state for over a thousand years. "From the reign of al-Mutawakkil to the reign of al-Muktafi; what has happened to one Caliph after another!" exclaims Ibn al-Tiqtaqah. "Murder, deposition, robbery—through the changed sentiments of his army and subjects. This one was blinded, that one killed, another deposed." Ibn al-Tiqtaqah, *Al-Fakhri*, trans. C.E.J. Whitting, (London; Luzac, 1947), p. 19. The influence of the army had increased rather than decreased at the time of the nineteenth century modernization movements which sought to convert armies into vehicles of modernization and change, as Turkey and Egypt illustrate. The Lebanese army developed around a small nucleus of five thousand men organized by the French during the Mandate period. Its officer corps was French trained and educated, a tradition which is still largely preserved. In spite of the growing tension in the Middle East the army remains relatively small, standing at about fifteen thousand.

17. On this theme see Arnold Toynbee, *The World and the West* (London: Oxford University Press, 1953), p. 22; On the role of armies in social change, see John Johnson (ed.), *The Role of the Military in Underdeveloped Countries* (Princeton University Press, 1962); S.E. Finer, *The Man on Horseback: The Role of the Military in Politics* (London: Pall Mall Press, 1962).

18. Islamic Law gives Christians and Jews autonomies under their respective religious heads, and, therefore, the rise of Islam Christian groupings in Lebanon have enjoyed a certain autonomy under their bishops who performed functions of both church and state. The Maronite Patriarch gained strength un-

der the French Mandate, while the Sunni Mufti gained power in the late 1950s as a result of the growing association of the Sunni community with President Nasser. The Shī'ī community, believed to be the "forgotten" community because of the poverty of its members, found itself united under the brilliant leadership of a young and dynamic leader, al-Imām Mūsa al-Ṣadr.

19. See Bishārah al-Khūri, *Haqa'īq Lubnaniyyah; passim.* Iskandar Riyāshi, *Qabl wa Ba'd* (Before and After) (Beirut: Hayat Press, 1953) passim.

20. The Communist Party was founded after World War I as an extension of the Palestine Communist Party. It has frequently been outlawed, but often reappeared under a new guise. While no communist candidate has yet succeeded in entering parliament, the Party exercises considerable influence on a number of trade unions.

21. *Ḥizb* (party) in Arabic tradition meant faction or dissent from the orthodox and enlightened community of believers. Parties (*aḥzab*) are attacked in the Qur'ān as groupings which have not seen the light, an unflattering association still strong in popular thinking.

22. The phenomenon of party leaders perpetuating themselves and constituting "a veritable 'ruling class' . . . that is more or less closed" has been noted by Duverger. "In theory," he writes, "the principle of election should prevent the formation of an oligarchy; in fact, it seems rather to favor it." Maurice Duverger, *Political Parties, Their Organization and Activity in the Modern State,* trans. by Barbara and Robert North, fifth printing (New York: Science Edition, 1967), p. 151; (London: Metheun, 1954); (New York: John Wiley and Sons, Inc., 1954).

23. Had the SSNP not been outlawed for long periods it would have provided a good example of the rise of a bureaucratic power structure after the death of a party leader. The leader of the SSNP was executed by the Lebanese government in 1949 after staging an uprising. The Party attempted another coup in

Lebanon in 1961, after which most of its leaders were put in jail. An amnesty was given them in 1969.

Chapter IV: Bureaucracy in Transition

1. For a useful guide to Middle Eastern bureaucracy see the pioneering study of Morroe Berger, *Bureaucracy and Society in Modern Egypt, A Study of the Higher Civil Service* (Princeton: Princeton University Press, 1957). The following two books by Adnan Iskandar and Iskandar Bashir were originally prepared as Ph.D. theses at the American University (Washington, D.C.) and Syracuse University (New York) respectively. Adnan Iskandar, *Bureaucracy in Lebanon*(Beirut: American University of Beirut, 1964); Iskandar Bashir, *Planned Administrative Change in Lebanon,* Raymond Nahhas, *Structure and Behavior of Lebanese Bureaucracy* (Unpublished M.A. Thesis, Department of Political Studies and Public Administration, Beirut, American University of Beirut, 1963).

2. In Lebanon the complexity of the bureaucratic system and the life-styles of the well-to-do are such that the well-placed citizen prefers not to deal directly with the bureaucracy, but sends his front men instead. A well-to-do Lebanese who needs to renew the license plate on his car can, for a tip, secure the help of a driver or mechanic to do the errand for him. No lawyer, engineer, physician, or banker would think of performing a transaction with the bureaucracy when an office boy or an unemployed cousin is available to do the task. This is one way to get around complexities and supplement the low income of the poorer classes. It provides the latter with opportunities to perform roles that add to their income, and, at the same time, makes life easier for those who can pay.

3. The reform committees of 1959 discovered a number of traditional bureaucrats who had no duties to perform. They came to their offices, chatted with their colleagues, and re-

turned home. Their jobs were expressions of gratitude for services to their political patrons. On the use of some ministries as dumping grounds for new employees favored by the "politicians," see Camille Chamoun, *Crise au Moyen-Orient*, (Paris: Gallimard, 1963), p. 247 and in passim.

4. The situation is perhaps most acute in Egypt, where literally dozens of coffee and messenger attendants crowd the corridors of any public building.

5. On the art of bureaucratic mystification see "Problems For the Front Office," *Fortune*, May, 1951.

6. This category includes a number of top men in the administration and the judiciary. A confidential report addressed by the inspectors in the Ministry of Justice to the Minister on August 2, 1965, states: "Teaching has become a second profession to the judges, and an additional source of income. His time which should be spent on his profession as a judge is being dissipated. . . . While the publication of books is one of his rights, he tends to use it for commercial purposes. The judge-author runs after the lawyers, the Ministry of Justice and the bookstores to sell his book and thus wastes his time in promotion for financial purposes and degrades his position."

7. This discussion depends heavily on the yearly reports of the Civil Service Council and of the Central Inspection Administration.

8. Officials, especially the highest ranking ones, usually have had legal training from Saint Joseph University. In 1952 the American University of Beirut began to offer B.A. and M.A. degrees in public administration and at times offered short-term, in-service training programs to members of the Lebanese bureaucracy and other Middle Eastern bureaucracies.

9. These deficiencies have been reported by the Central Committee for Administrative Reform, in *al-Taqrīr al-Thāni* (Second Report), dated March 23, 1959, pp. 6–14; see also Bashir Bilāni, "The Future of Lebanese Administration and its Devel-

opment" in *Al-Dawlah wa al-Inmā'fi Lubnān* (The State and Development in Lebanon), (Beirut: 1966), pp. 260 ff.

10. Buildings occupied by the bureaucracy are of five categories: (a) those inherited from the Ottomans, primarily military barracks, and including the largest and most stately buildings; (b) those built by the government to house certain ministries (Telegraph, Post and Telephone, Justice); (c) those such as the UNESCO building that were erected for a special conference and now are used by the bureaucracy according to need; (d) those rented from private owners, almost all of which are standard apartment buildings unsuited for the flow of work in a bureaucracy; and (e) villas rented from wealthy citizens to accommodate important offices of state.

11. Adnan Iskandar, *Bureaucracy in Lebanon*, pp. 32–33; with reference to confessionalism and public employment, Ṣā'ib Salām, (prime minister) has remarked that to the Lebanese, religion serves as a passport, a cheque, a privilege, and a certificate of competence. *Al-Jaridah* Newspaper, April 19, 1961, quoted by Iskandar, p. 33.

12. For a provocative study of bribery and its place in the development process see J. S. Nye, "Corruption and Political Development: A Cost-Benefit Analysis," *American Political Science Review* (June 1967): pp. 417–427.

13. The best account of the cynical attitude that pervades Lebanese bureaucracy and government is written by a prominent Lebanese journalist Iskandar Riyashi: *Qabl wa Ba'd*. Also see the yearly reports of the Central Inspection Administration.

14. Bashīr Bilāni, "The Future of Lebanese Administration and its Development," p. 258.

15. See Ralph Crow and Adnan Iskandar, "Administrative Reform in Lebanon, 1958–1959," *International Review of Administrative Sciences*, Vol. 27, No. 3 (Fall, 1961): p. 297.

16. The Law provides for three types of disciplinary councils, one relating to high-level bureaucrats, one for the employees of

the Foreign Office, and one for all other employees. These councils usually include the members of the Civil Service Council, inspectors from the Central Inspection Administration, and a judge.

17. The authority of the Central Inspection Administration extends to autonomous agencies, municipalities, and public schools.

18. The Council was originally begun as a private association; in 1962 it was given an official status, although it continued to operate autonomously under a Board of Trustees. The Board consists of prominent figures in Lebanese society.

19. One such suggestion has been for a National Council of Development, to be clearly modelled after the National Council for Tourism; another for a Cultural Council to deal with broad cultural matters in Lebanon. This suggestion is supported by the fact that the Ministry of National Education is essentially involved in administering teaching at the public school and national university levels and has no capability in promoting the broader cultural and artistic aspects of Lebanese society.

20. Beirut now covers 17 km^2, but is projected to extend from Dāmūr to Nahr al-Kalb to become known as Greater Beirut. Major government offices which are now outside Beirut proper, such as the Presidential Residence, the Ministry of Defense, and the Ministry of Public Works, would become incorporated into the new area. Bishārah al-Khūri Street, the public gardens in al-Sioufi and Burj Hammūd, and the Beirut Slaughter House have all been Council projects.

21. In 1969 and 1970 tension on the Israeli-Lebanese frontiers led to the evacuation of frontier villages in Lebanon and to a political crisis. The Shī'īs of the South under the leadership of Imām Mūsa al-Ṣadr declared a general strike and threatened to occupy the sumptuous villas in Beirut and its suburbs if the government did not respond to their claims, which included *inter alia* arming the villagers, strengthening military defenses

in the South, and compensating evacuees. The government formed this Council to determine how funds for the south, authorized by parliament, should be spent.

22. A High Judicial Body was established to investigate judges and a special organ set up to investigate the security forces.

23. Enabling Legislation.

24. See *al-Anwār* Newspaper, October 26, 1965.

Chapter V: Planning and Non-Planning

1. A brief survey of Lebanese planning is provided by Georges G. Corm, *Politique Économique et Planification au Liban 1953–1963* (Beirut: Imprimérie Universelle, 1964). The student of planning is advised to examine the numerous publications of Nadwat al-Dirāsāt al-Inmā'iyyah (Institute of Developmental Studies) in Beirut, which includes a number of prominent intellectuals and top members of the bureaucracy. The Institute holds bi-monthly seminars and yearly conferences on aspects of development and planning in Lebanon. Its publications include: *Modern Conceptions of Development in Lebanon* (Beirut, 1966); *The State and Development in Lebanon* (Beirut, 1966); *Development and Industrialization in Lebanon* (Beirut, 1968); *Man is the Capital* (Beirut, 1970). These publications are in Arabic.

2. The disparities are obvious in the studies prepared by IRFED and summarized in two volumes published by the Ministry of General Planning entitled *Besoins et Possibilités de Développement du Liban*. Etude Préliminaire 2v. (Liban, mission IRFED, 1960–61). A shorter, one-volume summation appeared in Arabic under the title *Lubnān Yuwājihu Tanmiyatahu* (Lebanon Faces its Development), (Beirut: Ministry of General Planning, 1963).

3. It included Maurice Jumayyil, Joseph Najjār, a graduate of the French École Polytechnique and a future minister of gen-

eral planning, and Jibrā'il Manassah, the author of the first comprehensive study on the development of Lebanese resources entitled *al-Taṣmīm al-Inshāʾī li al-Iqtiṣād al-Lubnāni wa Iṣlāḥ al-Dawlah* (Development Planning for the Economy of Lebanon and the Reform of the State), (Beirut: 1948), Jumayyil served as minister of General Planning in the last cabinet formed under President Ḥilu.

4. Head of l'Institut International de Recherche et de Formation en vue du Développement Integral et Harmonisé (IRFED), located in Paris.

5. Lebret started with the assumption that Lebanon wanted to develop but not at the expense of its liberal politico-economic system. He believed that "pseudo-liberty" in the public and private sectors would lead to anarchy. He espoused a degree of professionalism in both sectors and of cooperation to attain clearly defined objectives for Lebanese society as a whole. See his speech at the Cénacle Libanais, *Les Conferences du Cénacle* XVIIIe Année, No. 1, 1964, p. 37.

6. Jan Tinbergen, *Development Planning.* Trans. by N. D. Smith (New York: McGraw Hill Book Company, 1967), pp. 43–44.

7. At present all members of the Board are from the private sector and serve on a part-time basis. Professional and confessional qualifications are taken into consideration in their appointment. Half are engineers, four are economists, and one a professor of public administration. Six are graduates of French universities, and the others are from American universities. By confessions they are divided into three Maronites, three Sunni Muslims, one Druze, one Greek Catholic, one Greek Orthodox, and one Shīʿī. Reports published by the Board are poorly written and lacking systematic analysis and comprehensiveness. Unfortunately, its minutes, like most governmental businesses, are not published.

8. *The Five-Year Plan For Economic Development in Leba-*

non (published by the Ministry of General Planning, Beirut, 1958).

9. Actually urban planning had been going on since the early 1950s when Michel Écochard, a French city planner, drafted model plans for Beirut. Under the recommendations of the 1958 and 1965 Plans, 43 percent of the area of Beirut would be allocated to parks, roads, public buildings, and monuments—a Utopian vision in comparison to the heap of apartments, or "luxurious slums" (as Dean Raymond Ghusn of the Faculty of Engineering and Architecture of the American University of Beirut describes them) that now constitute Beirut. The 1965 Plan addressed itself to the planning needs of 23 towns and villages, with special attention to Tripoli, Sidon, Tyre and Zahlah. Lebanese urban plans list development projects in towns, and do not address themselves to cultural aspects of large cities. While Beirut claims numerous centers of higher education and bookstores, it still has no public libraries; those outside college environments cannot readily borrow books or find a place to relax and read. Although Lebanon is an archeological treasure, little of its past legacy decorates the streets, public buildings, and city squares. The capital of one of the most naturally aesthetic and archeologically rich countries in the world is itself aesthetically deprived.

10. Parliamentary minutes.

11. United Nations, *Studies on Selected Development Problems in Various Countries in the Middle East* (New York: 1967), p. 2.

12. Mr. Jumayyil was Minister of General Planning in the last Cabinet formed by Rashīd Karāmi under Charles Ḥilu.

13. *The Daily Star*, Friday, September 19, 1969, p. 5.

14. Basim Hannush, "The Present Socio-Economic Conditions in Lebanon and the Prospects for Economic Development," *Middle East Economic Papers* (Beirut: American University of Beirut, 1962), pp. 44-45. Hannush uses the word "plan" to refer

not to "a tightly regimented and controlled economy, but rather [to] a broad and comprehensive programme of action, free of internal inconsistencies, with a common purpose of development and a well-defined role of the public and private sectors in this common endeavor" (p. 45).

15. Statement by Premier 'Abdallah al-Yāfi before Parliament on April 27, 1966.

16. N. Raphaeli, "Development Planning: Lebanon," *Western Political Quarterly*, Vol. 22, No. 3, (Spring, 1967).

17. The Ministry has had two Directors General: Charles Tayyān, an engineer and member of the bureaucracy since the 1920s, and Muṣtapha al-Nuṣūli, an economist and former Director General of the Ministry of National Economy.

18. Such plants must meet certain conditions, such as promoting economic development and paying a minimum of L.L.100,000 in salaries to Lebanese employees.

19. A government decree to raise duties on a number of import items was introduced in the fall of 1971, but was immediately withdrawn when it was met by a general strike of the business community.

INDEX

'Abd al-Majīd, Ottoman Sultan, 9
agriculture, 47–50; and planning, 132–134
American University of Beirut, 9, 34–37 *passim*; medical center, 22; and agricultural development, 134
Annual Programs Service, 112
Apter, David, 26
Arab League, 141
Arab University of Beirut, 34, 37–38
Armenians, 24–25, 139; political parties, 25, 70; in Cabinet, 54
Ataturk, 25

Baghdad Pact, 27, 140
banking, 43; and industrial development, 47; attitude toward planning, 111
Beirut: as regional publishing center, 15; urban center, 31
Beirut Chamber of Commerce and Industry, 17
Beirut College for Women, 34, 35–36
Biqā' Plain, 19, 25, 132
bribery: in bureaucracy, 89–90
bureaucracy, 75–106, 144–145; defined, 75; under political formula, 75–80 *passim*, 105–106; stereotype officials, 81–84; reform in, 92–105 *passim*
business, 17; Club, 67–68

cabinet: and modernization, 13; under political formula, 54, 59–61; and development, 61–75; as head of bureaucracy, 77, 80; role in bureaucratic reform, 92–96 *passim*
Catholic Press, 36
Cénacle Libanais, 68
census of 1932, 20
Center of Higher Mathematical Studies, 34
Central Bank of Lebanon, 111
Central Committee for Administrative Reform, 94
Central Inspection Administration, 95–100 *passim*
Christians: attitudes toward modernization, 5–6
clubs, 102; role in presidential elections, 58; and political formula, 62–69, 73, 138
confessionalism: in education, 33–34, 39–40; in bureaucracy, 87–88, 95; as constraint on political formula, 138–139
Confessional loyalties: in 1860s conflict, 10; in 1958 conflict, 26–27; in 1969 Cabinet crisis, 27; and political power, 140
confessions: proportional representation of, 1, 14; European protection of, 11; groupings, 23–27; economic

disparities between, 44–45, 48, 51, 61, 109
Constitution, 11, 61–62; and political formula, 53, 55; on presidential power, 58, 102; on bureaucracy, 76, 88, 95
Constitutional Union Party, 70
consultants, foreign, 11, 16–17, 20–21
Council for the Execution of Major Projects for the City of Beirut, 99
Council for South Lebanon, 100

Deuxième Bureau, 64–65
Development Planning Service, 112
Directorates: Bidding, 97; Central Statistics, 112–113; Public Officials, 96; Research and Orientation, 97; Research and Planning, 112, 114; Training, 96
al-Dwaihī, Istfān, 7

Ecclesiastic Club, 65–66
economy, 40–51
Eddeh, Raymond, 65, 69
education, 7; Western-modeled, 1, 3, 9–10; higher, 34–38; pre-university, 39–40; reform in, 100; under 1965 Plan, 135
Egypt: invasion of Lebanon, 7–8
Eisenhower Doctrine, 26
election: law and process, 56–57
Embassy Club, 67
Emigration, 27–29; and economy, 44–45; of Maronites, 139
Europe: and modernization, 1, 6

Finance, Ministry of: and Planning, 114–115
Five Year Plan, 1958, 115–121, 126–134 passim
Five Year Plan, 1965, 111, 115, 121–135 passim
Ford Foundation, 93, 94
France: Mandate period, 1–2, 11–12, 20, 25, 70; and political formula, 52–55 passim

Franjiyyah, Suleiman, 61, 65, 143; and planning, 115, 128, 136
Fruit Office, 133

General Disciplinary Council, 95–103 passim
Green Plan, 132

Hagazian College, 34, 37
Hatti-Humayun, 9
Hatti-Sharif of Gulhane, 8
al-Hay'ah al Muwaḥḥadah, 100–102
Ḥilu, Charles, 65, 98; and bureaucratic reform, 95–105 passim, 145; and planning, 128, 134, 136
housing, 32–33
Hudson, Michael, 57, 58

Ibrāhīm Pasha, 8, 9
Industrial Development Council, 134
industry, 42, 45–47; and planning, 134
Institute for Administration and Development, 96
Institut International de Recherches et Formation en Vue de Développement (IRFED), 16, 21; and planning, 111, 121
Intellectuals: Club, 68–69; and planning, 109–110
Islam: as philosophical basis for modernization, 5, 6; political system under, 24
Istfān, Yūsuf, 7

Jesuits, 9, 15
Jumayyil, Maurice, 126–127
Jumayyil, Pierre, 65, 71
Junblāṭ, Kamāl: as za'īm, 13, 62, 63, 69; as party head, 71, 73
June War, 1967, 131, 134

Karāmi, Rashīd, 62, 94, 121
Katā'ib Party, 25, 26, 65, 70, 71
al-Khūri, Bishārah, 53, 98, 102, 110
al-Khūri, Michel, 98

Index

Lebanese University, 34, 36–37, 40, 131; under 1965 Plan, 135, 136
Lebanon: climate, 18, 19, 20; topography, 18, 19, 20; resources, 20; demography, 20–23, 31
Lebanon, 1958 conflict in: 26–27, 61, 94, 120, 143; and economic tension between religious groups, 48, 51, 110; role of za'īms in, 62; role of bureaucracy in, 89; as product of international forces, 140
Lebret, Father Louis Joseph, 110–111. *See also* Institut International de Recherches . . .
Liberal Party, 65
L'Orient, newspaper, 15

Maḥmūd II, Ottoman Sultan, 8
Maronites: influence on modernization, 6–7
media: influence on modernization, 10, 15–16
migration: rural-urban, 29–33 *passim*

military, 142–143; Club, 64–65
millet system, 26
missionaries, 8, 15; and education, 9, 33–36 *passim*, 40
modernization: defined, 2–3; and government, 2–3, 12, 75, 139–140; and political formula, 73–74
Mount Lebanon (Ottoman province): peasant revolts in, 7, 9
Muḥammad 'Ali, 8
Mukhtar: and village administration, 30
Murād, Niqūla, 7
mutaṣarrifiyyah regime, 10–11; and political formula, 51

al-Nahār, newspaper, 15
Najjadah Party, 26, 70
Nasser, Gamal, 27
National Bloc Party, 65, 70
National Liberal Party, 71
National Pact, 53–54, 58, 62

nepotism: in bureaucracy, 88–89

Office of Social Development, 99–100
Ottoman period: and modernization, 8–9

Palestinians, 21; refugees, 24–25; commandos, 27
Parliament: under political formula, 54–59 *passim*; and Cabinet recruitment, 60–61
Parliamentary Committee on Planning, 126
Permanent Civil Service Council, 95–100 *passim*
Personnel Law, 1959, 95, 96, 97
Planning: ministry of, 110–137 *passim*; Minister of, 128–129
Planning and Development Board, 110–129 *passim*
political formula, 4, 20, 52–74, 138, 139, 141, 144; defined, 13–14; and planning, 107–108; and modernization, 142
political parties: and political formula, 69–74
President, Office of: under political formula, 53, 57–61 *passim*, 143–144
Prime Minister, Office of: under political formula, 53–54, 59
Progressive Socialist Party, 71
Public Works, Ministry of: and planning, 114

radical elites, attitudes of: modernization, 14–15; education, 40; government, 55, 56, 59; political formula, 141, 142
Regional Activities Service, 112

Ṣā'ib Salām, 61, 62
Saint Joseph University, 9, 34, 36, 37, 81
Sarkīs, Eliyās, 65
Selīm III, Ottoman Sultan, 8
Shāhīn, Ṭānyus, 8

Shamʿūn, Kamīl, 13, 65, 71, 102, 110; in 1958 conflict, 26–27; and bureaucratic reform, 92–93; and planning, 111
Shihāb, amīr, 8
Shihāb, Fuʾād, 27, 64, 65, 102; and bureaucratic reform, 92–105 *passim*, 126, 145; and planning, 48, 110, 111, 128, 136
al-Ṣulḥ, Riyāḍ, 13, 53
al-Ṣulḥ, Sāmi, 93
Syrian Protestant College. *See* American University of Beirut
Syrian Social Nationalist Party, 70

tax structure: reform of, 134–135
Tinbergen, Jan, 111
tourism, 31, 45; and economy, 40–41; and development projects, 131; and private sector, 132
Tourism, National Council of, 98–99
Tripartite Alliance, 65
Tripoli International Fair, 131, 132

United Nations, 11, 141; and planning, 109, 126, 127
al-Usbūʿ al-ʿArabi, weekly, 15

villages: effect of modernization on, 29–33; economic disparities between, 48

zaʿīms: defined, 13–14; role in parliamentary elections, 56–57; Club, 62–64; and feudality, 63; and planning, 111; and modernization, 138; role under political formula, 139–141